Writing and Publishing Research in Kinesiology, Health, and Sport Science

Drawing on real-world experience and presented in an informal and accessible manner, *Writing and Publishing Research in Kinesiology, Health, and Sport Science* provides upper-level students and early-career academics with an essential resource to aid in disseminating research and publishing their first papers.

Logically structured to take researchers through each step of the publishing process, the book offers subject-specific advice on developing every aspect of theoretical, applied, or position papers, including:

- the title, abstract, and keywords
- method, results, and discussion sections
- referencing
- finding the right journal and submitting a paper
- revising content in light of peer review
- presenting papers.

This is important and accessible reading for any researchers seeking advice on publishing their work in fields including but not limited to kinesiology, health, exercise science, physical education, or recreation.

Timothy Baghurst is an Associate Professor in Health and Human Performance at Oklahoma State University, USA, and specializes in physical education and coaching.

Jason DeFreitas is an Assistant Professor in Health and Human Performance at Oklahoma State University, USA, and specializes in neuromuscular physiology.

Writing and Publishing Research in Kinesiology, Health, and Sport Science

Timothy Baghurst and
Jason DeFreitas

Routledge
Taylor & Francis Group

LONDON AND NEW YORK

First published 2017
by Routledge
2 Park Square, Milton Park, Abingdon, Oxon OX14 4RN

and by Routledge
605 Third Avenue, New York, NY 10017

First issued in paperback 2021

Routledge is an imprint of the Taylor & Francis Group, an informa business

British Library Cataloguing-in-Publication Data
A catalogue record for this book is available from the British Library

Library of Congress Cataloging-in-Publication Data
A catalog record for this book has been requested

ISBN 13: 978-0-367-37553-9 (pbk)
ISBN 13: 978-1-138-71592-9 (hbk)

Typeset in Times New Roman
by Apex CoVantage, LLC

Contents

Preface

It was 2001, and after three long, hard years of labor, I grasped within my hands a fresh, shiny undergraduate diploma. I'm not going to lie; I was proud of it. Four years earlier, as an 18 year old, I had no idea where I was applying or what I was applying for. In my ignorance, I was fortunate to have selected a university with an excellent reputation in my field of expertise.

As part of my degree program, research was a significant component. In fact, I was expected to complete an independent project, or thesis, to acquire my degree with "honours," and yes, that's spelled correctly. This was a major undertaking, and not all students completed the project. I did, however, and was accepted to present it at the discipline's national student conference. In sum, I was pretty pleased with my study and its findings.

Feeling confident, I began my graduate degree and decided that my study was worthy of more than just a presentation. My results were groundbreaking – to me anyway – and the journals in the field would surely clamber over one another to publish my study, right? It was in this frame of mind that I prepared and submitted my 17-page manuscript to one of the premier journals in the field before (im)patiently waiting for their response.

A couple of months later, I received an e-mail from the journal. I excitedly clicked it open, expecting to be covered in glory. The e-mail went something like this (serious paraphrasing here): "Dear Mr. Baghurst: We reviewed your manuscript and are rejecting it. Simply, it was awful. Included are reviewer comments explaining why it was awful. Sincerely, The Editor." I mentioned in the previous paragraph that my manuscript was 17 pages for a purpose. The reviewer comments explaining why my manuscript was so bad totaled 27 pages. I didn't speak for two days; seriously, I didn't.

If that was the end of the story, I wouldn't be writing this book. I was fortunate that a few months later, I met a professor willing to help me. We spent considerable time re-writing the manuscript, and he essentially mentored me through the process. I submitted the manuscript to a different journal, and following some minor revisions, my first manuscript was accepted for publication!

My point in writing this preface is to clarify that being published is not easy, particularly when working alone or without others who have extensive publishing experience. However, it can be done, and I hope that this book will help guide you through that process. How I wish I'd had this book when I first started!

I should also add that there are few things more exciting to me than getting a manuscript or book published. Over the past several years, I have mentored many first-time authors, and to see/hear their crying, screaming, and sheer joy at the accomplishment gives me tremendous pleasure. It's a great feeling, and I sincerely hope that by using my book, you experience the same pleasure.

– Timothy Baghurst, Ph.D.

Like Tim, I also lucked my way into a program with an excellent reputation in my field. For my undergraduate work, I simply went to the university that I was a childhood fan of (Go Huskies!), and for my graduate work, my wife and I selected the school that was closest to her family. Despite that the quality of program was not my top priority, I fortunately landed in great programs and have been blessed with excellent faculty mentors throughout my ten years of university schooling. I now strive to return the favor by mentoring graduate students on how to perform high-impact research, be published, and eventually become independent, successful scientists in their own right.

Tim is very well published in social-behavioral, educational, psychology, and sports science journals. Therefore, my contribution to this book is to bring other perspectives from different fields. I am an exercise physiologist by training and help run a neuromuscular physiology laboratory. As such, my publications are in physiology, neuroscience, biology, aging, clinical/medical, and human performance journals. Despite its popularity in the health field, I've never actually written a manuscript for publication in American Psychological Association (APA) format! Most journals that I publish in use American Medical Association (AMA) or some custom, journal-specific format. This is just one of the many differences between our fields. My area also has differences in the order of authors (and role of "senior/corresponding author"), the number of authors, the length of the introduction section, the format and depiction of the results, and more. This book is mostly based on Tim's experiences (including APA format); however, I have added interjections when the content of this book is drastically different in one of my health-related areas. Between the two of us, this book helps cover how to publish in most of the kinesiology, health, and sport sciences journals.

– Jason DeFreitas, Ph.D.

1   Introduction and assumptions

Some things within this book need to be clarified up front. Understanding what I am providing and what I'm assuming you've done already determines the success of this book. In other words, there are some things that this book won't solve for you, and I'm assuming that you have or can accomplish some fundamental steps that are necessary for you to publish successfully. Here are a few things that you need to note before you start this whole process.

1   I'm assuming that you have completed or intend (at some point) to complete a piece of writing that you wish to publish.
2   A journal will accept a variety of submissions (e.g., brief reports, data driven research, position papers), and I will discuss the main ones, but the book's focus will be directed toward empirically driven manuscripts where some form of data collection and analysis was conducted. I have also explained the various types and their layouts, but the primary content of this book assumes that you undertook some form of research study, such as a dissertation or thesis. If you haven't yet, that's perfectly okay, and perhaps using this book will help you prepare your research project.
3   I'm assuming that you're interested in publishing in the kinesiology, health, and/or sport science fields. That doesn't mean this book won't cover *a lot* of material that applies to many different fields, but it's more specific than a general text. In fact, I have included a chapter on writing theoretical articles just in case.
4   I'm writing with the understanding that you are submitting to a journal that requires formatting following the *Publication Manual of the American Psychological Association* (APA), 6th edition. That doesn't mean to say that this book is now worthless if you are not following APA, but Chapters 2, 5, and 6 particularly reference APA. Many journals have such bizarre and almost random formatting requirements that

it would be impossible to cover them all. Perhaps the most common are APA, AMA, Modern Language Association (MLA), and Harvard, but APA is going to be the focus. Therefore, the entire document should be written in Arial or Times New Roman (TNR) size 12. I prefer Times New Roman personally, and some APA journals will ask for TNR, so I recommend it over Arial. Again, this may differ based on the journal's own particular requirements, which are discussed more in Chapter 10.

5   Throughout this book, I've *italicized* tips that may help you simplify or organize your project. That's not to say that the rest of the content is irrelevant, but these are my own little suggestions that I've found helpful.

6   In addition to this book, the following article will be of help when working on your project: Cash, T. F. (2009). Caveats in the proficient preparation of an APA-style research manuscript for publication. *Body Image*, *6*, 1–6. For other referencing styles, a quick web search will pull up some useful guides such as Purdue OWL (https://owl.english. purdue.edu/owl/), which is a popular resource.

2 Layout

This chapter is integrally associated with Chapter 10. Each journal has its own formatting expectations, and therefore, while I'm going to provide you with a template, the formatting may need to be changed based on the requirements of the journal. If there is a particular journal that you know you are submitting to in advance, visit their website and find their submission requirements. They are often listed as "Author Guidelines."

Most journals will be very specific about how the manuscript should be written and presented. This is important to note. I serve and have served in both editorial and manuscript reviewer positions for journals, and I am much less likely to accept a manuscript that is not submitted in the correct format. My thinking is this: If the author was too lazy to check out the journal's expectations, were they lazy in their ethics, literature search, data analysis, or some other area? Simply, it places doubt in the reviewer's and editor's mind, which puts your manuscript immediately in a negative light. If the editor is undecided about whether to accept or reject your manuscript, this will probably help make the decision. Therefore, pay attention to the little details, as they may make the difference between your publication or your rejection.

Tip: Always, always, always save your work as a new file each time that you work on it. There's nothing worse than losing countless hours of labor because of a corrupted file (and it's happened to me!). I like to save each new file with the date I worked on it, so that I know which file I most recently edited.

In general, I recommend outlining the manuscript in its entirety before you begin. There's something about seeing all the headings and understanding where everything should be placed that helps to keep the manuscript orderly and organized. Now, some of these headings and "parts" to the lay-out of this manuscript will change when you submit it to a journal, but until that time, I recommend following my plan. It really helps to keep the manuscript organized and avoids the clutter of multiple files floating around your computer. Thus, your manuscript outline should look something like this (remember, this is a general APA format, but it won't differ greatly from other formats):

Relationship Between Motor Skill and Fitness: A Longitudinal Study

Timothy Baghurst, Ph.D.
Department of Quality Writing and Publishing
University of Academe
Publishing Town, QZ 12345

My other author(s) if appropriate

Direct Correspondence To:
Timothy Baghurst, Ph.D.
123 My Place of Work
Publishing Town, QZ 12345
E-mail: myemail@email.com
Phone: 123-456-7890

Abstract
(on its own page)

Title Again

Introduction
(don't actually include the word Introduction when you submit)
Various Headings May Be Appropriate
Study Purpose

Method

Participants

Instruments

Procedure

Data Analysis

Results

Various Headings May Be Appropriate

Discussion

Various Headings May Be Appropriate

References
Tables and Figures
(generally a new page for each table/figure depending on size)

Now let's break it down. On the first page, include your title in bold and centered. Under your title, include the author(s). Your title (e.g., Ed.D., Ph.D., M.A.) should also be included following your name. On the next line, include your working department followed by the organization on the next. This doesn't have to be an educational institution. Generally, it's the department where you work, but it doesn't have to be. For example, I recently worked with an author who was retired. We decided to include the school district he had taught at as his location. My co-author, Jason, chooses to use the name of his laboratory as his affiliation, which can be a useful way of marketing and promoting it to prospective students and perhaps future colleagues. Lastly, include the general address of the location (e.g., city, state, and zip code). Additional authors just go below.

Tip: If you have additional authors, I recommend including their e-mail addresses and phone numbers on this title page. You may not need them, but sometimes journals require the full contact information for all authors when you submit. Thus, getting it now means you don't have to wait on others when you're ready to submit your manuscript.

After the authors, include a "Direct Correspondence To:" heading. This doesn't all have to be on the first page. I once had a manuscript with eight authors, and it took three pages to get everybody listed with their contact information. However, someone should be designated as the corresponding author. Which author is designated as the corresponding author, as well as the order of authors, can vary quite a bit depending on the field. In the social-behavioral, or psychology fields, the authors are rank ordered strictly by their level of contribution. Therefore, the first author (also called the "primary" or "lead" author) performed the most work and would serve as the corresponding author.

However, in the physiology, biology, and medical fields, the first author may not be the corresponding author, and the last author has special meaning. The first author is frequently a graduate student who performed the data collection and worked under the guidance of a faculty supervisor to write the manuscript. The last author is the "senior" author, who presumably had a significant role in the concept/design of the study, had the lead role in analysis and interpretation, runs the laboratory that the study was performed in, mentored the graduate student that is the lead author, and may have even funded the study (through grants). For this reason, the last author might be the individual that is actually recognized in the citing of their work. For example, consider the following sentence in which Dr. William Kraemer would be the senior author on this cited work, "Recent work out of William Kraemer's lab (e.g., Flanagan et al., 2016) showed . . .". Therefore, in these fields, the senior/last author serves as the corresponding author. Regardless of which field you're in and which author order you use, note that only individuals that had a significant contribution to the study or manuscript should be included in the author list.

Your abstract then goes on the next page. This will be detailed more in Chapter 3, but just create the heading in bold. Then, on the next page repeat your title at the top in bold and centered. I also include "Introduction" in bold beneath the title just as a reminder, but it is not required according to APA, and I remove the heading before I submit. I simply find it useful as a reminder when I'm building my manuscript. Note that the title is the last time that you must begin on a new page. The remaining headings simply follow however they fit in the manuscript and do not require starting on a new page. I usually give a few spaces between them initially, however, just so they're spaced out.

Within the Introduction, Results, and Discussion, you may have subheadings, and what they are will depend on what you're writing about. However, with respect to the method section, there are several subheadings that are pretty much standard for APA research-based manuscripts. They may differ slightly depending on what kind of research you're doing (e.g., qualitative vs. quantitative), but they should appear on the left in bold. More about that in Chapter 5.

Results, Discussion, and References should all appear in bold and be centered. Again, they should *not* begin on a new page unless they naturally fall on a new page, or when you've completed your final manuscript, they end up at the very bottom of a page with no text underneath. I highly recommend acquiring the APA 6th edition if you don't have it already and you plan to write more in APA format. If this is a one-time project (for now at least), there are several good websites that will assist you with APA expertise. More about that in Chapter 9.

Tables and figures don't get their own heading, but they should be placed at the end of the manuscript after the references. They used to be required within the text, then we were required to put them at the end of the text and "indicate" in the text where they should be placed, and now we're just required to place them at the end of the document.

Tip: I struggle to write about the contents of my tables and figures when they're at the end of the document and I can't see them. Therefore, I do one of two things: (a) because I have two monitors, I paste them into a separate document in the second monitor so that I can see my results while I write, or (b) when I don't have a second monitor, I simply put them where they "belong" in the text and then move them to the end when I'm done.

Eventually tables and figures need to go at the end, and there's no specific heading for them. Each table and figure goes on a separate page unless they're quite small. The editor will merge them into the text once the manuscript has been accepted. Many journals may ask for figures to be uploaded separately as image files. This allows for higher-resolution figures for publication.

3 Title, abstract, and keywords

It would be an understatement to say that your title, abstract, and keywords are important. They're crucial, and with software increasingly responsible for sorting information, they are becoming more and more vital. The title is important because it attracts the reader to the topic. The abstract determines whether the reader wants to commit the time to reading the whole thing. Also, database software will search the title, abstract, and keywords when a user is looking for a particular topic. If these three elements are unclear or poorly presented, that one prospective reader who really needed to see your article is going to miss it. Therefore, take some time to get this right. Too often authors will hurriedly write the abstract (and keywords in particular) without spending too much thought on it, which is a mistake.

Title

The title is everything. It's what determines whether your reader is going to read anything else about your study. The classic testament to this fact is attending poster presentations at a conference. Attendees will wander around reading the titles only. If the title attracts them, they will stop and at least read a little more. If it doesn't, they smile and continue or avoid the dreaded eye contact and quickly move on.

In general, my preference is to provide a working title to my manuscript, but not add in the keywords and abstract until it is complete. You don't have to do it this way, but I find it helpful. I need some kind of working title in order to direct my thought processes. For example, the title is the first thing I wrote when I started this book. I changed it three times in the first hour. That's okay, as a title can evolve, but it certainly helps to have a starting point.

The title needs to be something short enough to be read, but long enough to get a few keywords in place that might attract readers. It's easier said than done. The title has to be carefully thought out, which is why I change my own titles so much. Last year I wrote up a manuscript about a piece of research some colleagues and I completed. We also got the opportunity to present this study at a conference, and after doing so, I hung up the poster in the hallway outside my office along with many others. It's been fun to watch students and faculty walk down the hallway and stop what they're doing to read about this study.

It's the title that stops them: "The Effect of Music and Musical Genres on Putting Accuracy in Golf." Why do people stop at *this* poster over all of the others? Well, there might be a few reasons.

Tip: Just because you completed a research project with a specific title (e.g., an ethics approval or dissertation title) doesn't mean that you have to use that title for your manuscript.

---

1   Someone can quickly read the title as they're passing. It's relatively short. Imagine the title "The Performance Effects of Listening to Five Differing Genres of Music on the Putting Accuracy in Golf Practice Among Division I Collegiate Golfing Men and Women." Wow, that's a mouthful! In passing by, the casual reader didn't get finished with the title and therefore moved on, missing out on this great study! Therefore, be careful that your title isn't too long.
2   Your title can't be too short either, as your prospective readers simply might not find it. Consider "Music, Putting, and Golf." It doesn't really tell the story of what we were trying to find out. Yes, it might still attract someone to read, but it really doesn't tell us too much about the study.
3   Your title also needs to include keywords that your reader will recognize and find interesting. Let's stay with the golf title. Why do so many people stop at this one poster? Well, the poster is hung in the health and human performance department, which is housed in the university's wellness building. Golf is a popular sport in the area (the building also has an indoor putting green and virtual driving range), and most people passing are interested in and listen to music. Therefore, the title is reaching a specific audience. When you create a title, it has to pique interest.
4   The title shouldn't be overly complicated. Yes, having a complicated title makes it sound as though you're intelligent and know what you're

talking about, but it also means that some people won't read it for fear that they won't understand it or it won't apply to them. How about "Cacophony or Rhythmic Modulation? Impactfulness of Musical Flavors on Golfing Performance in Singular Strokes on Greens: A Randomized, Controlled, Multi-gender Study." Not only did this title sound pompous, but I also managed to apparently create a new word (*impactfulness*) and make it a very, very long title. The additional danger of such a title is that while your study might have real-world applicability, it's presented in such a manner as to dissuade the "average" person from reading it. Therefore, someone who might be very interested in reading and sharing your work to a broader audience, like a journalist, might not take the time to read it.

5   When writing a title, you need to focus on the key elements of your study. For example, if your sample isn't really, really important to the outcome of the study, then don't include it. The exception might be when you've studied a very specific group such as children with cerebral palsy, for example. In the golfing example, that the participants included both collegiate male and female athletes is important, but it's not essential to the title.

To summarize this section, here's another example of a title for a manuscript that I recently had published. "Effect of a 14-Week Program to Reduce Employee Risk Factors for Metabolic Syndrome (MetS)." There are a few key things I wanted my audience to know. First, 14 weeks is important to the study. Second, the aim "reduction" is included. Third, the key variable "Metabolic Syndrome" is included. Finally, the term MetS is included for those searching for the shorter version of Metabolic Syndrome. I included MetS, not because other studies in the field have, but because I believe that over time, researchers and writers will begin using the shortened version. I don't want my article to be missed by their searches!

Abstract

From my experience working with other writers, a good abstract is perhaps the hardest component of the article. You've attracted the reader by the title, but really, the abstract determines whether they'll read it. I struggle with abstracts too, primarily because journals can be very restrictive with word length. I once had a journal limit my abstract to 50 words. By the end of this sentence, I've already reached 75 words in just this paragraph! Therefore, it's extremely important that you get every word right. It's amazing how succinct you can be if you have to.

Tip: Don't forget that APA requires no indent on the abstract. It's a common mistake, but getting it right shows your attention to detail that reviewers and the editor will like.

A research abstract (theoretical abstracts are discussed in Chapter 8) is designed to provide an overall purpose, methodology, results, and conclusion to your study. In essence, it's a summary. You can't fit everything in there, so you have to decide what key components of each aspect need to be included. Some journals will expect you to include headings in the abstract, but most don't. However, it makes sense to write the abstract as if it had headings. This will aid the flow of the abstract.

Here's a guide using the concept of the "Relationship Between Motor Skill and Fitness: A Longitudinal Study" title used in Chapter 1. In this example, I used a quantitative design, but later I'll show you how it might look with a qualitative design.

1   Using one or two sentences, state the problem and purpose of the study. "There is some evidence to suggest that developing sport-based motor skills in adolescence leads to improved physical activity levels in adulthood. This study sought to determine the degree to which motor skills in adolescence could predict adult fitness levels."

2   Next, state who your participants were and what they did. "Participants were 165 male and 143 female high school students of mean age 16.8 years ($SD = 0.9$) from three schools in an urban area of a Northern state who completed the Test of Sport-Based Skills. After 20 years, 98 males and 84 females from the original sample were located and completed the Adult Physical Fitness Test, which measures cardiovascular fitness and muscular strength and endurance."

Tip: APA frowns upon using sources in an abstract. The exception is when you're referring to a measure, which then should be referenced. Other reference formats expect it. Check with the journal you're submitting to and read some of their submissions for examples.

3   What you found comes next and can be lengthy or short depending on what research design you used. The key aspect here is that you include

only the most important findings, otherwise this section becomes too large. Report the main finding (your purpose) and then one or two "interesting" ancillary findings that readers may find interesting. "The Test of Sport-Based Skills was found to be a strong predictor of all components of the Adult Physical Fitness Test." Note that some journals will expect you to include the statistical notations for the findings in a quantitative design, but others prefer that you don't. Not all journals state what you should do. I prefer to leave them out, as many of the numbers don't tell you much without the context. However, I do encourage at least including the p value (don't forget it should be in italics!) to provide the level of significance. Again, check some journal examples to see what the norm is.

4   You're now ready to present your discussion and conclusion. This needs to be quite brief and limited to a sentence or two. If you have research to support or refute your findings, then a sentence can be included highlighting this. Even if this is a novel topic, and many studies tend to be, then mention of similar studies or findings can be included. Irrespective, in this section you're addressing the "so what" component of your study. How will this study make a difference? "Therefore, programmers such as physical educators should consider encouraging skill development in high school populations if participants are to be more physically fit as mature adults."

The whole abstract is included at the end of this section so that you can see what it looks like in its entirety. In total, it's 152 words long, which would fit well below the 200–250 mark of many journals. However, if a journal requires 150 words or less, there are one or two words that can be eliminated or sentences written differently to be more concise. My recommendation is that you write the abstract, include everything you want to, and then cut it down if that's what the journal requires.

Tip: I always work on a manuscript in a general folder that I consider the master document. However, when I'm ready to submit a manuscript, I save a new copy in its own subfolder, in addition to the documents associated with a submission. Then, if the manuscript is rejected and the new journal I wish to submit to has different standards, I create a new subfolder and repeat using the original master copy. For example, let's say that I have a master manuscript with a 250-word abstract, but the journal requires 150 words. I save the manuscript to the subfolder and cut it down. Then, if that manuscript is rejected and I have to resubmit to a different journal that wants a 250-word limit, I don't have to re-write the abstract back up to 250. This is similarly applicable for complications like formatting, where one journal requires AMA and another APA. You do not want to have to change your manuscript from AMA to APA only to later have to change it back to AMA for a different journal!

Complete abstract

There is some evidence to suggest that developing sport-based motor skills in adolescence leads to improved physical activity levels in adulthood. This study sought to determine the degree to which motor skills in adolescence could predict adult fitness levels. Participants were 165 male and 143 female high school students of mean age 16.8 years ($SD = 0.9$) from three schools in an urban area of a Northern state who completed the Test of Sport-Based Skills. After 20 years, 98 males and 84 females from the original sample were located and completed the Adult Physical Fitness Test, which measures cardiovascular fitness and muscular strength and endurance. The Test of Sport-Based Skills was found to be a strong predictor of all components of the Adult Physical Fitness Test. Therefore, programmers such as physical educators should consider encouraging skill development in high school populations if participants are to be more physically fit as mature adults.

A qualitative example

A qualitative design does change the abstract, but not greatly. Essentially, your method and results are likely to change. Rather than take you through systematically, I've provided another abstract example using the same ideas so that you can see how it changes from a quantitative approach. Note that there are many different qualitative designs along with a variety of ways to report the findings, but in the present example, I conducted interviews and sought themes.

There is some evidence to suggest that developing sport-based motor skills in adolescence leads to improved physical activity levels in adulthood. This study sought to determine the degree to which motor skills developed in adolescence were perceived to influence adult fitness levels. Participants were a convenient sample of 16 males and 11 females (*M* age = 38.6 yr., *SD* = 0.9) from an urban area of a Northern state who had been raised in that region. Following a pilot using six participants, the remaining sample were invited to complete one of six, 60-minute focus groups where they were asked questions associated with the topic in a semi-structured fashion. Questions were pre-determined based on grounded theory, but participants were encouraged to extend their answers through follow-up questioning. Findings revealed three main themes of sport experiences growing up, family support for physical activity and sports, and access to resources. Findings indicated that the provision of community sports activities along with the support of parents during adolescence was crucial in fostering sport-based motor skills that led toward greater participation in physical activity as adults. Therefore, programmers need to consider how best to utilize the facilities available, while engaging the parents in the process of developing sport-based skills among adolescents.

When to write the abstract

This may seem like a strange heading at first. I imagine that most people would immediately assume that the abstract should be written at the beginning of the writing process. There's nothing wrong with writing the abstract first, but I prefer to leave it until the very end. Regardless of whether I'm converting a completed dissertation to a manuscript, writing up a research project for the first time, or developing a position paper from scratch, I always feel like I have a better understanding of the manuscript at the end of the process than at the beginning. Therefore, I recommend waiting until you have completed the manuscript before attempting to write the abstract.

Keywords

Keywords are used in search engines and are therefore crucial in attracting readers to your article. If your keywords are too broad, they will get lost in the search; likewise, if your keywords are too specific, they will limit potential readers. Therefore, it's important to take a little time to get them right.

Generally, journals will expect about three to five keywords that are *not* part of the title. Take the study already mentioned: "Relationship Between Motor Skill and Fitness: A Longitudinal Study." Keywords that are already used in the title don't help. What three to five keywords would be appropriate here? Words like *fundamental motor skills, motor learning, physical activity*, and *gross motor skills* might all be applicable. They're not in the title, but they are still relevant to the topic.

I like to put my keywords (separated by semicolons unless specified otherwise by the journal you're applying to) immediately following the abstract, but a few journals require them on your title page. Some journals allow you to choose any keywords you wish, while others expect you to make a selection from a pre-determined list. Either way, listing your preferred keywords before you begin the submission process makes it a little easier to submit when the time comes.

4 Introduction of the manuscript

While reading this chapter, recognize that this section is being written on the understanding that you've conducted some kind of research project that you wish to be published. Although in my opinion (and I'm a little biased), you'll learn something from every section in this book, if you're writing a theoretical/ position paper or a science-based applied article for practitioners, then I've provided a section later in this chapter just for you; however, it doesn't include some of the material in this section that may still be important to you.

General guidelines

As you've read articles surrounding your topic, you should have gotten an idea of what's expected in the introduction. As the title implies, you should be expected to introduce the purpose of your research, and it sets the scene to your study. It's a careful reporting of the work that has occurred in the past that highlights the need for your study. This is typically done in a three-stage process (set the scene, present past research and theory, purpose of the study), which we'll get to a little later in this chapter.

Headings

Note that headings within the introduction are acceptable. In fact, I like using them to help keep the introduction following a logical progression. Also, as a reviewer, I like headings in the introduction just because they break up the text. It's a personal preference, but a several-page introduction without headings can get quite boggy.

Tip: Before I begin writing my introduction, I have a general idea of what I intend to write. Therefore, I create headings within my introduction before I begin writing. It helps to focus my writing. I can always change the wording of my headings, just like I can and do with my title, but they provide direction. Otherwise, my writing tends to be a little aimless.

There's no set page limit to an introduction. It's important not to overwhelm the reader with an unnecessary review of literature, but simultaneously, the reader needs to understand that you've done your homework and presented a case for your study. I find it the hardest section. In general, however, anything from four to six pages of text double-spaced is quite normal. Again, this is a flexible number and may depend on what specific discipline you're in.

If you've completed a dissertation and are looking to rework it, this may be the hardest part of the process. How do you get your dissertation's introduction and lit review, probably 30 pages or more of content, into just a few pages? After all, you wrote it into the dissertation because of its importance right? Well, unfortunately, you can't include it all, and you have to be clinical in making cuts. My recommendation is that you take the majority of the introduction from your dissertation, and then take choice work from your lit review. You won't be able to take much, so make sure it's the key literature that will support your purpose. Remember that everything in the introduction is designed to lead toward why your study is so important.

Quotations

In general, quotations are frowned upon within an introduction. It's okay to have quotations, but they should be limited to just one or two key quotes. Determining what is a "key quote" is up to you, but in general, it's a seminal component of an article, for example, that really nails down a point you're trying to say. In other words, only use quotes when you absolutely have to or you simply can't write it any better. Most novice writers rely too heavily on quotes.

Here's an example. Recently I was writing about a particular topic where I was highlighting the inadequate empirical research to date. I provided a few examples of studies that were lacking, but I needed something extra to drive home my point. Fortunately, I found an author who stated almost word-for-word what I was trying to state. Quoting those few sentences was a perfect way to state my case.

Tip: Remember that in APA, quotes above 40 words have to be set out differently to your normal text. This can visually interrupt the flow of the manuscript. Therefore, unless the quote is just amazing, try to find a way to keep that quote below 40 words so that it can stay within the normal textual format.

Writing style

Writing should be in the past tense when referring to an author's thoughts, opinions, and findings. It's very important to be consistent in your writing, and when you're referencing past research, it should be written in the past tense or a variant form. Therefore, avoid inserting the use of present tense verbs even when it might seem appropriate. For example, "Baghurst (2017) suggests that . . ." Because "Baghurst" isn't in the present tense, a better way of citing this would be, "It has been suggested that . . . (Baghurst 2017)" or "Baghurst (2017) suggested that . . ." Thus, this common mistake can be easily corrected.

One of the only situations where present tense might be appropriate is when referencing a theory or concept. The theory itself, while created in the past, technically exists in the present, too. Consider these two examples to understand how tenses change:

1   "In his theory of physical activity levels, Baghurst (2016) posited that . . ."
2   "The theory of physical activity levels posits that . . ."

In the first example, the sentence is built around the author, whereas in the second, it is focused on the theory.

An additional consideration when writing the introduction, and sometimes in the discussion as well, is the use of interpretive words that may not be appropriate. It's important not to read too much into what an author is attempting to convey. If we do, we tend to make statements that simply aren't true, or even if they are, we can't back them up. Perhaps the most commonly seen example is the use of "argue." I regularly see this word when reviewing manuscripts and other academic writing such as dissertations. However, how do you know that the author you're citing is arguing? Unless the author actually states that he or she is arguing, you have made an assumption. It's quite a strong word!

The use of the word *argue* is a common example, but writing an introduction needs to consider both existing facts and unknowns. Therefore, unless an author categorically stated something, you have to be careful about being declarative and using words that leave no room for maneuver. To avoid this, read your work and carefully consider the verbs that you're using. I'm a big fan of inserting words that provide some wiggle room such as *may, could,* and *might* when trying to make points, especially when I'm referring to a theory or gap in the literature. It's perfectly okay to state what an author found in his or her study, but it's the interpretation of these findings that requires some finesse. Consider the following two approaches:

1 "Baghurst (2017) reported that not all of the participants adhered to the program, which impacts how these findings are interpreted."
2 "Baghurst (2017) found that not all of the participants adhered to the program, which may have impacted the study's overall outcome."

Both of these examples are true, yet the second one provides a softer approach and allows the reader to form his or her own conclusion. In the first example, there's no room for doubt. I've declaratively decided that adherence *did* impact the findings. However, in the second example, I'm accepting that it may or may not have impacted the findings. It's a slight but important difference.

Tip: When I was a graduate student, I was once told by my professor that no one cared about my opinion because I had no "status." Rather, if I had an original thought, I should find the works of others and use them to convey my thinking. Harsh, but that has stuck with me, particularly when writing an introduction. Leave your own thoughts and perspective until the discussion.

Part 1: Set the scene

In the first stage, you're expected to set the scene. Let's say I wanted to investigate whether having physical education classes every school day reduced the body mass index levels of school children. Not exactly the greatest research idea, but we'll just play with it for the purposes of this book. The first thing I would need to do is present facts concerning obesity levels in the United States before detailing facts that are more specific to the group I was going to investigate. Readers need to know that obesity is a problem; otherwise, what's the point of the research?

The theoretical background or perspective is also an important consideration to add. Note that this isn't a requirement for some journals and it is for others. Most won't tell you whether this is expected, but you may find that an editor or reviewer comments on a lack of theoretical background in the introduction. However, in general, qualitative studies and journals that focus on qualitative research are more expectant of a theoretical perspective than quantitative work.

This is a difficult area to explain, in part because everyone has his or her own opinion about what *theoretical background* actually means. The purpose of this section is not to explain this topic in detail, but essentially, as a reviewer once explained to me, everyone has a position from which they are coming from, and it needs to be understood by the reader. In essence, you're expected to explain what theories or background you are basing your perspective on.

To make it very clear, I recommend that you consider including a "Theoretical Background/Perspective" section in your introduction, particularly if you know that the editor/reviewer will be expecting it. Again, this isn't a "must include" in your introduction, and most of my research does not include this section, but particularly for qualitative studies, a perspective should be provided.

Part 2: Present past research and theory

The second step would be to present *select* findings associated with the topic. Following with the example that I've been using, I would present research associated with physical education and weight reduction. I need to show the readership that I've done my homework, that this is a topic of interest to people, and that there is nothing out there like what I'm planning on doing. This allows me to show what we do know, but also highlight what we do not. In other words, it is a chance to identify the gaps in the literature. It is important to present some of the flaws or inadequacies of the current research, particularly if I'm "correcting" those issues in my own study (or "filling the gap"). Thus, continuing with this example, I would definitely discuss the differing strategies to reduce obesity in children, the physical effects of daily activity, and any similar studies that might support justification for undertaking my own study.

I used the term select because in many situations, there might be a myriad of articles that you could include. An introduction need not include the 100 articles that a literature review of a dissertation might. In fact, some journals will limit the number of references you're allowed to use, but don't worry about that until you submit. It's fairly easy to cut out a few references if need be. Essentially, within the introduction, you're providing the readers with the best, most relevant information for their edification.

I recently worked with a co-author to publish the findings of her dissertation. To her horror, in working on the manuscript, she discovered an article that had been published with a similar sample and research topic! However, this isn't a bad thing, and I had to explain this to her. You see, just because someone else has done something similar doesn't mean your work is futile. Yes, ideally, this article could have been used to influence the course or betterment of the dissertation, but it can be used to your advantage. Reading their article allowed us to find weaknesses or differences in their study that highlight the purposes of our own.

Another tricky part about writing this section is that it is important to show the inadequacies of the existing literature *without* coming across as attacking it. For example, my co-author Jason utilizes a technique of soft language that stresses what is new or what is being added by his research without accusing the previous literature of being "wrong." He frames his research as a follow-up study to previous work. Taking a hard tone with past research may cause those authors to send a letter to the editor defending their work, and often attacking yours in return (and these petty battles often become less about the science). Letters to the editor are often published and linked to the research article that it is responding to. Therefore, carefully consider the consequences of the tone you use when pointing out what is missing in past research. Consider the following examples,

- **Example #1 – Too Harsh:** "Jones et al. (2015) showed that. . . . However, these authors failed to consider the potential differences in *Variable X* between various populations."
- **Example #1 – Better:** "Jones et al. (2015) showed that. . . . While this study was a good starting point, it is important to see if differences in *Variable X* exist between various populations (e.g., age, ethnicity). Therefore, the purpose of our study . . ."
- **Example #2 – Too Harsh:** "Smith et al. (1997) showed that. . . . However, their methodology is outdated and no longer considered sufficient to examine *Variable X*."
- **Example #2 – Better:** "Smith et al. (1997) showed that. . . . While Smith et al. (1997) utilized state-of-the-art methods at the time, technological advancements have allowed us to examine *Variable X* with more accuracy and reliability than ever before. Therefore, the purpose of our study . . ."

In the first example, the better version acknowledged the past research as a good starting point and shaped the current paper (i.e., your research) as a follow-up study to further enhance our understanding. In the second example, the better version acknowledged that the past researchers did the best they could with the technology available at the time, and again shaped the current paper as a follow-up study (utilizing the advanced technology). All of the examples above show inadequacies (or the need for more research), but the better versions do so without being confrontational.

Remember, you may (more than likely) see these other authors at conferences or even job interviews in the future.

Part 3: Purpose of the study

The final portion of the introduction should be to lead smoothly into the purpose of the study. You've described the general rationale, you've discussed the importance of this topic and the holes in the current research, and now you finally get to state the purpose of your study. You may also take a sentence or two to explain how the findings of this study might be useful.

Whether you make a heading for your purpose or not is entirely up to you. If my purpose, which might include several hypotheses and research questions, is lengthy, then I tend to create it as a new heading in the introduction; however, it's not always necessary.

The purpose is usually limited to one or, at most, two paragraphs. The key in presenting the purpose is to follow a few simple steps. Note that I'll use my hypothetical study of physical education and body mass index levels to provide a practical example:

1   In a couple of sentences, summarize what we currently know against what we don't. "Regular physical activity has been shown to reduce or maintain the body mass of adolescents. However, it is unclear whether participation in physical education classes regularly would serve to lower the body mass of participants, as there is evidence to indicate that participation in physical activity outside of the school environment is the greatest predictor of body mass."
2   State the overarching or primary purpose of the study. You may have more than one, but I prefer to state the primary purpose, and then if there are additional purposes, they are considered secondary. Some people prefer to consider each purpose as equal, but in all my research, there was a specific goal I was trying to achieve. Everything else was interesting, but not as important. However, it's entirely up to you. "Therefore, the purpose of this study was to . . ."

Hypotheses and research questions

It's not usually required by a journal to include the stated hypotheses or research questions, but I do recommend it. It just clarifies to the reader exactly what you're looking to explore. In some cases, depending on the number of questions you're looking to investigate, this can be helpful in the discussion. If I'm exploring several ideas, I like to address them one-by-one in the results and discussion sections so that my questions in the introduction, the answers in the results, and the explanations in the discussion are all tied together neatly. Of course, this doesn't make as much sense if there are only one or two questions to be addressed.

Whether you use hypotheses or research questions is entirely up to you. It depends on the topic and whether your introduction dictates making a legitimate estimation of what might happen, or whether your study is more exploratory in nature. But it's one or the other, not both.

Tip: Theses and dissertations generally require you to include null and alternative hypotheses as well as research questions. Those preparing a manuscript in this situation will commonly include all of them, but only one (i.e., null or alternate or research questions) is required.

I like to finish the introduction by stating the hypotheses or research questions within the study purpose section. If you've written the introduction well, then when the research questions and hypotheses are stated, they should make sense. In other words, they shouldn't suddenly introduce a new concept or variable not discussed in the introduction. If you do, a good reviewer will be sure to question why you're introducing this now, when it's never been discussed before. For example, if one of your questions introduces an exploration of gender differences, the introduction must have discussed this as a relevant topic first. By the time your reader gets to this section, there should be no surprises, and this section should easily transfer the reader into the method of your study.

The length of the introduction

It's important to note that the length of the introduction section is highly dependent on the field and journal. It was mentioned earlier in this chapter that the introduction can be a "few pages." The APA-based journals typically expect a lengthy introduction allowing a detailed "Theoretical Framework" to be established. I have had introduction sections as long as seven double-spaced pages before. However, the physiology/medical journals typically expect much smaller, more concise introduction sections. Presuming the paper is an original research article (and not a special topic review or meta-analysis), an introduction in these types of journals is likely not to exceed two double-spaced pages. In fact, my co-author, Jason, has received negative feedback from reviewers regarding his introduction being "too long" when he exceeds only four paragraphs.

The introduction section in physiology journals has the same flow as the three sub-sections mentioned before (i.e., 1. Set the scene, 2. Present past research and theory, and 3. Purpose of the study), but each section is squeezed into its own paragraph (and no more). In these journals, you can't afford to talk too much about the important studies in the introduction. Instead, make general statements, cite any important articles, and then discuss those articles in more detail in the discussion section (where you might compare their results with yours). Writing this section can sometimes be as stressful as having to write a very short abstract. For the physiology journals, you have to be parsimonious (frugal) with your words, and concision becomes an important, learned skill (the more you write, the better you get).

5   Method

Assuming that you've already completed a study, presenting the methods in a logical and detailed manner are crucial to making a reviewer and editor happy. If you're preparing a study such as a thesis or dissertation, note that this is one area that you can't mess up! Many, many things can be changed in a manuscript, but if you messed up the data collection, it's not something you can go back and fix. There is nothing worse than figuring out your study had a fatal flaw after the fact.

For example, I was recently asked to provide feedback at a graduate student poster session at a national conference. In reviewing the study, the student had collected data at two points in the middle of programming rather than at the beginning and end. The result was that the data couldn't be used to evaluate the effect of the programming even though this had been claimed in the title. This was not something readily fixed, and consequently, publishing the results were now in serious jeopardy. Lesson to be learned: methodology cannot change ex post facto.

Journals will require you to follow their own guidelines for the layout of the manuscript (see Chapter 2), but in general, you should use headings similar to Participants, Instruments, Procedure, and Data Analysis. Journals may ask you to combine headings or change them slightly, but working with these headings from the start provides a generally acceptable format. For experimental studies with a repeated measures design, it is also common to have a "Study Design" sub-section first, prior to the Participants. This provides a foundation for the reader to understand the overall design (e.g., time points of data collection). If the design is complicated, this section should also include a figure that provides a flow chart of the study design.

A key aspect of the methodology is providing enough detail for the study to be replicable. This is a fundamental flaw of many manuscript submissions, as they lack the detail necessary for a reader to clearly understand who was investigated, what measures were used, and how they were delivered. Without detail, the reader is left wondering, which is not what you want your reviewer or editor to be doing! Set the tone by providing detail, which can always be eliminated if they choose to recommend it. It's much better to be in that position than have many questions from reviewers who are confused about the methodology.

Tip: Ask someone familiar with research but unfamiliar to your study to read through your methodology. Ask them to repeat back how you conducted the study. It should help locate any holes or address any questions that a reviewer unfamiliar with your study might have.

Participants

Participants are whom you studied. Many times, authors attempt to include too much information into this section. While it is okay to provide some general information on where the participants were acquired, remember the procedure section explains how they were acquired. Your responsibility is to outline who they are.

How much demographic information you should include in this section is debatable. If you have a long list of demographics, they may be more appropriately placed in the results section. However, you want your readers to have a fundamental understanding of who you were researching. How many participants did you have? Male or female? Ages? Ethnicity? Were they a specific group (e.g., have asthma, completed an educational program, have a knee injury, are trained athletes)? What was their educational status? There is a myriad of demographic questions that might help provide a picture of your participants, but what you include really depends on what your study is. These are just general demographics that you'll see in most journal articles. Here are a few typical examples of participant descriptions that were recently published across different journals:

Example 1: Participants were 22 (8 male, 14 female) Caucasian volunteers from two men's and women's Division I golf programs from the Midwest United States. Participants were on average 20.3 ($SD =$ 0.81) years old and were enrolled as full-time students with a minimum of eight years of golf experience. Prior to the study, participants were required to agree to IRB conditions.

(Baghurst, Tapps, Boolani, Jacobson, & Gill, 2014)

Example 2: Participants were obstetrical patients between the ages of 20 and 25 who gave birth at a hospital located in the Western United

States and planned to breastfeed their infants. In addition, participants had delivered a normal, single infant, at least 37 weeks gestation with a birth weight above 2,500 grams, and had no severe medical conditions or complications. Women participating in WIC and mothers who planned to exclusively bottle-feed were excluded from the study. Ethnic background, race, and religious preference were not specified; however, all participants had to be able to read and speak English in order to read the consent form and receive lactation follow-up calls via telephone.

(Eichmann & Baghurst, 2015)

Example 3: Participants were 169 individuals at a 4-year institution in the United States with a PETE program in which students could become certified physical education teachers. Programs such as 2-year institutions, kinesiology programs that did not have a PETE program, and programs that did not lead to licensure were excluded from analysis. Participants were solicited from their university website as being responsible for directing the program; however, it was requested that the survey be passed to another if that person was not best able to answer questions (e.g., the person was department head, but did not have a physical education background or did not directly oversee the physical education program).

Two websites (www.A2ZColleges.com and www.petersons.com) were used to develop a master database of PETE programs nationwide. Users may use these websites to search for academic programs by state. Academic institutions that were reported to possess a PETE program were entered into a master list, and the two websites were cross-referenced to check for institutions that may have been overlooked with just one source. The master list comprised 592 universities, and 195 participants representing these programs began the survey yielding a 32.94% response rate.

Participants who indicated their university did not have a PETE program, did not have a program that led to licensure, or did not complete the entire survey were eliminated from further analysis, resulting in 169 usable responses. Participants were not required to identify their institution unless they wanted to opt out of receiving a reminder e-mail or receive synopsis of the results. Almost two-thirds of the sample (61.13%) identified their educational institution, and all states were represented. Of those that participated, 106 indicated that they conducted fitness testing in their program, whereas 63 participants indicated that they did not fitness test.

(Baghurst & Mwavita, 2014)

As you can see, these three examples are very different and contain very different information, yet all were accepted for publication. Notice in Example 1 that not too much detail is given beyond basic demographics. It is interesting to note that mention of the Institutional Review Board (IRB) is made here, but it is more commonly seen in the procedure section. In Example 2, it is clearly explained how participants were selected, yet other demographics were not collected, which is something that a reviewer or editor might comment on. A failure to obtain these demographics might be tempered by the more sensitive situation. Example 3 is much more detailed because it was important to clarify how these participants were located and who actually completed the survey. Example 3 is also an online survey compared with a telephonic survey in Example 2. Consequently, a response rate is provided as well as exclusionary criteria to ensure that the responses were from those who should be responding to the survey. Therefore, much more detail about the participants was needed.

In some situations, multiple groups of participants might be included, such as comparisons between groups, for example. In this case, consider writing a paragraph for each, or, if there is simply too much information, a table might be a better choice.

Instruments

The instruments section details what equipment or techniques you used to gather the data. This section varies a lot depending on your research design. For example, conducting interviews versus doing a VO_{2max} test will result in very different components required in this section. Irrespective of what you're using to measure, you must detail the protocols or rationale for using it. For example, if you're measuring body fat, how are you measuring it? If you're using a survey, was it self-designed or one previously created by someone else? If conducting interviews, how were the questions developed?

The key in this section is demonstrating that whatever tools you're using have been carefully selected and will measure what they're supposed to measure (i.e., they're valid), and ensuring that enough detail has been included to explain how these tools are useful. Details need to be included such as the equipment's use in other studies and the instrument's validity and reliability scores, or details of the pilot study and expert input used to develop the interview questions. No examples are provided here simply because the instrument section can become quite lengthy, but ask yourself if your data collection method is completely clear to your reader and if you have clearly explained why this equipment or method is the most appropriate.

Procedure

Your procedure should detail exactly how you obtained your data. You've already recounted whom you worked with and what you used to get the data, and now it's time to explain in logical order how the data were obtained. Usually it makes sense to describe the chronological order in which you obtained the data. It should be a progression from the beginning to end. It's quite common at the beginning of this section to mention your ethics approval. It makes sense, as it's usually the first thing you need to do to begin your study.

Many journals are becoming fussier regarding the IRB statement, often requiring that specific declarations are made (such as "consent was obtained" and "this study was approved by an ethics committee"). An example of a more thorough IRB statement is, "All subjects were informed of the experimental procedures, risks, and their ability to withdraw from the study without penalty before signing consent. This research was conducted in accordance with the Declaration of Helsinki and was approved by the university institutional review board." Note that the specific university that approved the study was not stated. This is because many journals use a double-blind peer review process, and the reviewers could potentially piece together who wrote the paper if specifics were included.

There are things that are not necessary to include in the procedure, such as when you purchase equipment, or how long it took you to develop your survey, but sometimes time is important. For example, if you're conducting an online survey, how long did the survey remain open? Some authors choose to include specific dates or times in their manuscript. For the most part, it's not necessary unless it has specific relevance to your study. Examining physical activity levels of a community in July versus December might require you to be more specific, or if your data are focused on a specific point in time such as the Olympics, dates become more relevant. Otherwise, stating that data were collected from May 15, 2016, to October 24, 2016, doesn't really tell us much.

Tip: If you're struggling to get your procedure down, bullet point in sequence what you did in order to get your data. Then write those bullets into sentences and paragraphs.

Data analysis

The goal of this section is to explain how your data were analyzed (remember that *data* is plural!). Some of this may be a little redundant, especially for statistical analysis, when it's repeated in the results section, but it also shows you're able to synthesize how you analyzed your data. Depending on your type of data, this section could range from very small to very long (largest section of the paper). For example, Jason's neuromuscular lab often measures biomechanical variables, which includes the processing of electrical signals such as force, velocity, and EMG (i.e., muscle activity). The processing of these signals can become quite complicated, and many questions need to be answered to adequately describe it, such as how signals were filtered to remove noise, which section (or chunk of time) of the signals were analyzed (e.g., the moment the participant landed from a jump), and how the variables were calculated.

Other areas of physiology might also have very lengthy data analysis sections. For example, describing how blood samples or tissue samples are processed can be a lengthy process to describe. Remember that the point of your method section is so that someone else could replicate your study if they so choose. Therefore, if you performed a complicated analysis, then be sure to thoroughly explain how it was done. It can also be useful to break down your data analysis if you have multiple methods of analysis. It's almost preparing the reader for what is about to come!

In qualitative studies, you typically are expected to explain the theoretical and/or systematic way in which you acquired your results (often presented as themes). Within this section, you may be expected to detail how you made sure that your data were reliable and valid. What you include is very much dependent on what the journal's expectations are, but generally, it's better to list more than less. You can always cut it down, but you don't want a reviewer wondering whether you collected and analyzed data accurately.

Tip: Converting qualitative theses and dissertations into articles of a manageable length can often be particularly challenging often because they're generally longer. Data analyses sections in theses and dissertations tend to be overkill, and it's unlikely you'll need to include so much rationale for your analyses in a manuscript. It's actually one area where you might be able to save a little space that can be used for your results, which are typically much longer.

6   Results

A common mistake that many authors make is including interpretation within their results. Your results should be just that: a presentation of what was found. There should be no additional details that add the author's opinions to the actual results. That's what the discussion is for! You might see a combination of results and discussion in the same section, but it's very rare, and usually a qualitative study.

What sections you create in your results section will vary greatly depending on what you researched. It's not really feasible to identify common headings, but I often use the hypotheses or research questions as headings. If you don't have many results to report, you may not necessarily need headings at all. It's mentioned in Chapter 9, but if your data are better presented in tables and/or figures, then do so.

Sometimes, especially when converting a thesis or dissertation into a manuscript, you have more results than you can include in an article. Again, you need to refer back to what your research questions and hypotheses are, and make sure that those are answered. There's no need to add in extraneous findings that detract from your overall theme. Demographics are a good example of this: you may have collected a lot of demographics, but many of them may not really be important to your findings.

Quantitative results

Quantitative results, in my opinion, are much easier to present than qualitative results (or they are at least more straightforward). Often tables and figures can be used to keep the results section succinct. Generally, it's best to start the results either in order of statistical complexity, easier to harder, or in order of research question. Statistical notations are expected in this section, and how you present them will vary depending on manuscript style.

With any style, statistical notations need to be presented consistently; it's important. No reviewer wants to see mathematical notations randomly arranged. Again, this leads back to asking how careful the author was in designing, collecting, and analyzing the data. A clean, crisp results section indicates professionalism and confidence.

Tip: Be sure all of your notations are defined somewhere in your text.

Qualitative results

Not surprisingly, qualitative results are presented differently. Generally, results are presented as themes that emerge from the data either by coding-using researchers and experts or by using software. Themes are generated and are then presented with supporting quotes or evidence from the content.

How you order your themes is not set, but if you can lay out your themes in some kind of logical order, it makes sense to do so. For example, in a recent focus group study, I presented the themes according to how they fit into the chronological order of the participants' experiences.

Themes should be supported by at least one piece of evidence from your investigation. I also recommend more than one just to show that it's not a one-off example. In situations where you might have conducted an interview or focus groups, I would expect you to have included examples from all or almost all participants. Sometimes authors focus too heavily on one person, and while that person may have a lot to say, the reviewer needs to know that more than just one person shared the theme.

Tip: If you already have a journal in mind, check out the layout of their qualitative studies to see what they do and don't do in the results section. Some journals will have very specific requirements about how qualitative studies are presented, and it will save time later if you are writing it to their specifications.

Qualitative results can get very long very quickly, especially if you have many themes and subthemes. Add two or three quotes to each description of each theme, and suddenly, you're looking at pages of results. It really eats into your page length. Be succinct with the quotes and cut out sections wherever possible. Instead of including someone's entire 80-word statement, for example, try and cut out the irrelevancies and focus on the one or two sentences or phrases that really get at what you're trying to convey.

7 Discussion

There are a variety of ways to present a discussion, and like anything written, the author's style is going to differ. However, there are some general guidelines for writing a discussion that I recommend at least considering. There's no magic solution to developing a great discussion, but here are some general suggestions that I have found to be most successful.

Overview

Sometimes manuscripts are quite lengthy and can contain several areas of investigation. Consequently, before I delve into the discussion section, I use a paragraph to remind my reader of the article's purpose(s), and then spend a sentence or two highlighting the main outcomes of the study. This sets up the discussion and ensures that the reader hasn't forgotten what my study's overall purpose was, and it summarizes the results section.

Discussion of the results

The discussion is named such because it should be discursive. It allows the author to extrapolate a little on the findings and confirm or reject what has been found previously. It should be something that reflects on what has been found, compares it to what others have found, and reaches some new thoughts or conclusions.

Now this is no simple task, and it can be easy to get near the end and rush through the discussion. However, the discussion should be written carefully, as it's essentially the first time you are permitted to deviate away from what has been done in the past and what has been found in the study. Now you get an opportunity to speculate a little and perhaps write something meaningful for your audience. In other words, take your time and get it right. Discussions are great places for other authors to pull quotes from your work because it's fresh thinking.

Since the discussion is the area of your paper that is the most "quotable," you have to be careful as to how much you speculate. Don't make grandiose statements that could never be supported by evidence. Limit your speculation to hypotheses that could potentially be answered in future studies. For example, consider the following statement, "We are unsure why our findings differed from those shown by Smith et al. (2012), but it is possible that it is due to the populations used. Our participants were well-trained athletes, while theirs were sedentary individuals." In this example, explaining the differences in findings as a result of different populations used is speculation, but it is testable speculation. If someone were so inclined, he or she could replicate your study, comparing athletes versus sedentary individuals.

The format of how results are discussed is up to you. There are no set rules. I usually present findings in the order the research questions were presented at the end of the introduction and results section. You don't want to confuse the reader by jumping around in each section of the manuscript. In a qualitative study, I'd stick to presenting the themes in the same order as the results. In each section, present one or two key findings that are then compared to previous research. This usually allows for an opportunity to speculate about what it could mean or how it could be interpreted.

Limitations and future research

This is sometimes forgotten within the discussion section, but it's important to recognize that no research study is perfect, that you're aware of your study's imperfections, and that you understand that future research is possible based on your findings. Some authors will split up the limitations and future research into two sections, but I like to combine them. After all, shouldn't the limitations create holes in the research that could be explored in the future?

> Tip: I generally start this section by combining both limitations and future research within one sentence. For example, I'd say something like, "There are limitations to the study that provide opportunities for future research."

Don't get too critical of your research. You know your study better than anyone, and it's easy to be overly critical of what you've done. Instead, focus on two or three weaknesses. Don't think there are any? Ask another student, professor, or colleague to read it. I'm sure they'll find a few. The point is to address the main issues. It shows the reviewers and editor that you understand your research has flaws but that you also understand how to correct them.

Future research is just that. It's an explanation of where your study can be taken next. It could be extending what you've done, experimenting with different demographics, or using different resources. Ultimately, this is an opportunity to guide your readers into potentially researching something you have questions about yourself. You could be directing other researchers into your own area of research!

Tip: If you have plans to continue in this line of research, then try to work in to your discussion how this research could be expanded further. For example, you might mention that it would be useful to investigate a specific group. Then, when you work on your next project, you can cite the present article that indicated that it was recognized as an area needing further research!

Application and conclusion

Some journals will expect an application of your findings, whereas others will not, and they will just require a conclusion. I'm a big proponent of applied research. How does your work make a difference? If there is no application section, then application can be presented in the main discussion section when you break down your findings. Otherwise, it can be presented here. I find this to be a very meaningful section and one that is very important to a reviewer. Reviewers want to know the "so what" to your study.

This, as well as the conclusion, shouldn't be too long. You're really just summarizing what was found and what it means. There might be mention of future research, or how this research can be applied. Choose the last sentence in your manuscript carefully. You want your reader to be left with something tangible and meaningful. Of the many, many articles I have reviewed, the ones that make me think for a few days (or longer) are usually the ones that end well. They provide the proverbial food for thought. Ending with a fluffy, wordy, and meaningless sentence does little good in that respect.

8   Theoretical, applied, or position papers

This chapter is included because not all articles are, or indeed need to be, research-focused. These are considered to be theoretical, applied, or position papers. Theoretical articles tend to propose a new theory or something similar. There are even some journals that are entirely dedicated to this type of paper, such as the journal *Medical Hypotheses*. Applied articles tend to take the results of research, or perhaps even a theory, and develop some kind of practical application from them. Position articles tend to make a declarative statement in some form or another. It's usually presented as an opinion piece whereby the author is making a case for something. Many times, position statements come from multiple authors from across different academic institutions and countries. This helps make a bigger statement.

There's no specific format for writing these types of articles. My suggestion is to plan what you're going to write using key headings before writing in the rest. Remember that it should be a logical progression through the manuscript to lead to the applications, model, or position you're trying to make. In your own research, look at how other papers similar to the one you're proposing are formatted. Investigate some of the theoretical papers written in journals you think are potential homes for your article to see how they are set out. There's simply no common method for the layout of these articles.

What makes your article special?

Irrespective of what kind of non-research article is being written, the editor and reviewers will expect some "special sauce." This is how it was once explained to me, and how I'm going to pass it on. A special sauce refers to the "something" in the manuscript that makes it different to anything else already out there. That's one of the big problems with trying to get literature reviews published: they don't really do anything except save a researcher the time and effort to do it himself or herself. Rather, to be seriously considered, your article has to add some new perspective, thought, application, or methodology to what is currently known and understood. It's a hard thing to do, but it gives you the best chance of getting an article accepted that has no new data to add to the literature.

What can special sauce be? Here are a few examples. In one article, I took the results from my dissertation, expanded on an article that had already been published, and explained where researchers needed to focus their attention in the future. In another article, I wrote a position paper explaining a philosophy that practitioners were currently following and why I thought it was wrong, and then I provided an alternative perspective. More practically, some colleagues and I took the current literature in a field, pulled out specific findings for a select group, and then demonstrated how our knowledge of this group could lead to practical applications to improve how we work with them.

Now these are all just general examples, but they show how something new can be written from existing literature, but there has to be a continuation of what is currently understood. There has to be something that the reader takes away that is *new*, rather than re-hashing old material. That is the biggest criticism made of non-research articles. You have to answer the "so what" question that will be posed by editors, reviewers, and readers alike.

It should be noted that these types of papers should not be your first attempt at publication. These papers have significantly more impact if they come from an expert in the field rather than a novice. However, once you've published a couple articles on a topic, you'll have established enough credibility on that topic to attempt a paper of this nature.

Tip: If you are a novice and do want to write something like this, make sure you work with an established author in the field with credibility in that area. It will help to solidify that your work has the approval of someone well recognized and respected, and it will likely be taken more seriously by editors and readers.

9 References, tables, and figures

References can be an absolute pain if you don't follow a few simple rules. Not taking care to do the references well also suggests to the editor and reviewer that you might be a little hasty and careless in your work. As a reviewer, I *love* it when an author has taken the time to get the references right. It makes it so much easier to review, as I don't have to address that section. Here are several things to consider when working on references.

1   Write your article in the format you're most familiar with. For some, it's going to be APA, but for others it will be AMA or something else. It doesn't matter really, but writing in the referencing format that you're most familiar with will make your writing flow better. You'll spend less time thinking about how to reference something and more time writing.

2   Decide at the beginning whether you're going to use reference software. There is a variety out there, and while I'm not going to get into the merits of each, the more common ones are usually more common for a reason. The *huge* advantage of reference software is that your manuscript can be easily transferred between one format and another. This is really valuable if your writing crosses over disciplines and if reference styles are going to vary. Switching referencing styles manually is a very time-consuming process.

Tip: Don't trust the referencing software to get it right. Often, they just pull the reference from an online index, and it's wrong in the index! This means that if you don't check your references, there will sometimes (more often than not in my experience) be mistakes within the referencing. Therefore, even if you let the software do the bulk of the labor, check all of the work!

3   Personally, I'm old school and do my referencing manually, which is more time consuming, but I know it's done right and I don't have to double check software. Most will tell you to go for the software. It's hard to argue otherwise.

4   Use online search engines and journals to help you. Often, they will have the citation format you need, and it can just be copied and pasted into your references or uploaded into your software. This saves a lot of time, but recognize again that mistakes are often made and that you should double check them. *Index Medicus* is a good search term if you're looking to find journal abbreviations. University libraries as well as many online sources have tools to help you cite correctly. Even though I have my APA manual nearby, sometimes it's faster just to visit a trusted referencing site for a quick check of a rule.

5   Don't make the mistake of including references in the text but not including them in the references until later. In a writing flow, you may be inclined to add them later, but it's awful if you cite some author from some article you now can't find in your stack of articles or saved in that folder somewhere on your computer. Now you have to search online to find the article based on maybe a name, a date, and some contextual information. It is far, far better to take the couple of minutes to get the reference written up. This will save a lot of time in the end. In addition, it's no fun thinking that you're finished only to remember that you have hours of reference writing and checking to do.

6   Don't get lazy on references. I already mentioned the perspective of the reviewer, but it's easy to overlook the reference section, and doing it right can really influence how a reviewer sees your work.

7   Double check that references in the text are in the reference section and vice versa. When making many edits to a manuscript, it can be easy to add or delete a reference from the text, but not the reference section (advantage if you use software). To double check, print off your manuscript and create a separate reference page(s). Then as you go through the manuscript, check off the citations in the reference section; any that aren't checked off by the time you finish are not cited in your manuscript. You can double check by searching those names in your computer document.

Tip: Make sure you search variants of the author's name or more than one author. It may be that you misspelled the first author or perhaps you got the author order wrong in the manuscript. It's worth double checking so that you don't delete them from the reference section only to discover they are indeed in the manuscript.

8   Finally, and this is *very important,* don't cite an article simply because it was cited the same way in another paper. Find the paper that you wish to cite, read it yourself, and confirm/validate what was said before you go on record saying the same thing. You'd be surprised how often articles are incorrectly cited. I frequently see an interesting citation, go read that article, and then think to myself, "that's not what that study showed at all."

Tables and figures

Tables and figures are (or should be) straightforward. They should be used when the data you are presenting are better understood in a visually attractive format versus written within the text. Also, use a table or figure if the content is lengthy; no one really wants to read lines and lines of data in a paragraph.

How tables and figures are set out varies by referencing method and journal, but when writing the manuscript, almost all journals request that you include them at the end of the manuscript and not within it. I usually write my manuscript with them *in* the text and then move them when I'm finished. This helps me see what I'm writing about rather than having to scroll back and forth.

You can certainly overdo the number of tables and figures in a manuscript, but a few often go a long way to keeping the manuscript's length down. The key is to include what you need but not over-clutter them with unnecessary information. Simpler is usually better.

Figures can be made in various software, but the most common are graphs, and Microsoft Excel is quite efficient at making clean and good-looking graphs. SPSS and other statistical software can also make graphs, but they sometimes have less functionality and don't allow you to edit as much.

The table function in Microsoft Word (or any other writing software) should be your friend. I've worked with authors who have opted to present their tables using the tab function or counting out spaces, but this gets messy when the editor wants to convert the table to their specifications. Don't do it! Table formats will vary by journal and referencing, but you can and should design your table logically, which is what most editors and reviewers will want to see. The key difference between referencing styles is usually the title of the tables and figures.

Tip: I create my tables with all of the lines in the table to see the breaks between rows and columns. I remove the unnecessary lines at the very end.

When deciding how to present your data, there are a few things to consider that might help make your decision. If the values themselves are important (e.g., to be used as normative or reference data for a population), then the data should definitely be presented in a table so that the reader has the exact values. However, if a comparison is the purpose of your research (e.g., between time points, conditions, or groups), then a figure might be a better option. A figure makes it easier for the reader to visualize the differences between those time points, conditions, or groups. When utilizing a figure, be sure to include vertical error bars to show the variability (standard deviations) of the data. Also, be sure that all of your axes are appropriately labeled, including the unit of measure.

Tip: Don't rely on color for comparisons unless it is imperative. Most journals will print in black and white only or charge extra for color figures. Therefore, I always look at my figures on the gray scale to make sure all of the comparisons can still be made. Using different lines (solid vs. dashed), data markers, or shades of gray in the bars can help.

It is important to note that almost every journal prefers that data not be repeated unnecessarily. Therefore, data can be presented in the text, in tables, or in figures, but don't present the same data in multiple formats. Choose your presentation format and only present it in that manner. However, some data can be in tables, while different data are in figures (just not the same data in both).

Lastly, like it or not, there will be many readers that only read your title and your abstract, and look at your figures without ever actually reading the paper. Therefore, I was taught that figures should be able to "stand alone" and be separate from the manuscript. What I mean by this is that the figure tells its whole story, and the reader doesn't have to refer to the method or results section to understand the table or figure. To accomplish this, it's important that the caption or legend sufficiently describes what the table/figure shows, and it should define each abbreviation used. If all of the description is in the text of the results, then the reader may miss it when viewing the figure. Consider the following figure caption from Jason's thesis (2009):

Figure 1: The mean thigh muscle cross-sectional area (CSA; cm^2) and isometric maximum voluntary contraction (MVC; N) from the first testing session through the 8 weeks of training. P1 and P2 are the two pre-testing sessions. W1 – W8 are weeks into training. The vertical error bars represent standard deviations.

* denotes statistically significant difference ($p < 0.05$) from P1.

In this example, the first sentence acts as the title for the figure (albeit a very detailed title). From that sentence alone, without any reference to the paper, the reader already knows (1) this was an eight-week training study and (2) which variables were measured. All of the abbreviations (MVC, CSA, etc.) are defined, including the time point labels on the x-axis (P1, P2, W1, etc.). Symbols are defined (e.g.*), and units of measure are included (cm^2 and N). As a result, almost everything that a reader would need to understand the figure is included, without having to go back and forth with the text (i.e., the figure and its caption "stand alone").

10 Finding the right journal

Not every article is publishable, but just because an article is rejected the first time doesn't mean it isn't publishable. A lot depends on finding the right journal for your article. More than once I've had an article rejected within an hour of submission because the editor did not think that it fit the scope of the journal. Finding that fit isn't easy, but it's a lot easier when you have a good article! Here are some pointers to get your article in the right journal.

Choosing your target journal

There is a plethora of journals out there. There are so many of them at times that it's hard to comprehend! It's important to find one that is visible in your field. Yes, I've been published in some less-than-stellar journals, but it was usually when I wasn't first author or I was at wit's end and just wanted it published. Not ideal.

Rather, you need to look at journals you're familiar with. If you're familiar with them, then chances are you're hearing about them from other academics or students, or you are reading articles from them. That's usually a good first sign.

> Tip: I often go through the reference section of my article and look for journals that might pop up more than once or twice. If I'm referencing them, then they're probably going to be interested in a similar line of research.

I would also encourage you to submit to the best journal that you think your article can be accepted in. Sometimes, I've been pleasantly surprised that a journal has taken my article when I thought it would be rejected. You just never know. That being said, don't be overly ambitious. Weak data hidden under the guise of a well-written article isn't going to fool many. In general, start high and work your way down.

Contacting the editor

Sometimes you might find a really good journal, but you're just not sure whether it is a good fit. At times, I have sent a brief e-mail to the editor in which I include the title and abstract of the article and ask for their opinion. Sometimes the editor will be frank and encourage you to look elsewhere; other times, the editor may encourage a submission. Sometimes the editor won't write back at all, which is probably a sign that your article review is going to take a long time! Most times it gets you a quick answer rather than wasting a few days waiting for an editor to automatically reject it.

Contacting the editor is not something I make a habit of, but it can be useful if you're really not sure about the article's fit with the journal. It can also be useful if the journal has a submission fee attached. You don't want to pay to submit to a journal only to have the editor reject it outright because it wasn't considered a good fit!

Open access

Open access journals are those that allow everyone to read your published article without any kind of subscription. Essentially, the idea here is that if your article is open access, it will be read and subsequently referenced by more people. That may be true, but it may also be false. Most people who will read your peer-reviewed article are probably going to be academics who have access to the journal through their library somehow anyway.

Many journals now offer the opportunity to pay an open-access fee so that everyone can read your work. Some journals automatically have their journal set as open access, which is nice, but you're probably already paying for the privilege. Really, it comes down to whether you're willing to pay the fees, which are often hefty, to make your article open access. Philosophically, Jason and I don't believe that scientific work should be hidden behind some subscription-based paywall (i.e., most journals). However, our recommendation is that you shouldn't pay for open access. We've yet to see any hard data supporting the benefits of the investment (e.g., greater number of reads or citations).

Indexing

Which journal you should publish in should be moderated by who you want your audience to be and how much exposure you want. Indexing is hugely important. There are a variety of different indexes in which journals have their work listed, and each will have idiosyncrasies or specialize in particular areas. Some big ones include SPORTDiscus, Medline, PubMed, Academic Search Premier, PsychINFO, ERIC, and HealthSource. There are many others, but these give you an idea. Google Scholar is also something to include, as it can be a useful resource to find articles, but it's a little less specific, perhaps a little less regulated, and it isn't as user friendly as databases with more specific search options.

Ideally, you want your journal to publish in one or more of the main databases so that other scholars can find your article. Not getting indexed means that your work is very unlikely to be found or read. Checking that the journal is indexed and where it's indexed should be one of the first things you do.

Impact factors

Loosely defined, an impact factor is a number that evaluates how often a journal or article has been cited over the course of a year. In theory, the higher a journal's impact factor the more times its articles have been cited.

Journals with impact factors, and especially those with high factor numbers, are considered good because they show that the journal is being well-read and cited. Some academics consider them very highly, and if you can get published in a journal with a high impact factor, that doesn't hurt at all. Often journals with impact factors will state their score on their website, or sometimes a simple web search will pull it up.

Recognize that just because a journal doesn't have a high impact factor, or that it doesn't have an impact factor at all, doesn't mean you shouldn't consider it. Many fields (e.g., psychology) have many journals with impact factors, whereas others (e.g., physical education) rarely have journals with impact factors. It doesn't mean that PE journals aren't read or cited, but that the publisher may have elected not to acquire an impact factor. Acquiring an impact factor is not a simple task and is not free: sometimes publishers evaluate the cost-benefit of acquiring one and decide against it.

As an author, you have to evaluate whether it's truly important to be published in journals with an impact factor. It's more important that the journal's indexed than that it has an impact factor. You also have to evaluate who your target audience is. Here's a good example: recently I had an article published in a PE journal. By the year's end, it was the most downloaded article for that year (over 1,000 downloads). However, it has never been cited, and if the journal were to acquire an impact factor, I'm sure that my article and the others in the journal would keep the factor very low. This is because the journal is a practitioner journal, which means its readership aren't writers or citers (i.e., they aren't typically researchers). It all comes back to one question: Who do you want to read your article? In this case, I wanted practitioners to read and apply my work, and it wasn't important if anyone cited it (although it's always nice when it happens!).

My recommendation when it comes to impact factors is to talk to others in your field to solicit their input. Some disciplines put no stock in them, whereas others may not "count" your publications in journals without them or journals that don't have a high enough impact factor.

Predatory journals

Understand that a journal that is open access and requires a publishing fee does not make it a predatory journal. More on that later. A predatory journal might be defined as one that exists with the sole purpose of making profit without particular care or interest in ensuring the quality of its publication. Many of these have cropped up over the past decade as a business model disguising themselves as authentic journals or publishers, saying all the right things, but in reality, lacking academic rigor in their process for publication. It's really important to do your homework on the journal you want to submit to.

There is no obvious way to find out if a journal is considered predatory, but there are a few things to at least check:

1   Check Beall's List which is now archived (https://web.archive.org/web/20170112125427/https://scholarlyoa.com/publishers/). Unfortunately, this list was discontinued in 2017, but it remains a valuable resource. Note that they state this list is for "potential, possible, or probable predatory scholarly open-access publishers," and so it isn't an inclusive or exclusive list. However, it's a good guide that I use every time I consider submitting to a journal that I'm not familiar with. Note also that it references the *publisher*, not the name of the journal, so if you're interested in the journal, you need to determine its publisher. Consider searching for key words such as "predatory journals," as new sites may be developed.

Tip: I made the mistake once of allowing a primary author to handle all submission decisions only to find out later that the author had submitted and had been accepted to a journal published by one on this list. It was an honest mistake, and the primary author had had no idea. Make sure that if you're co-authoring an article that you're aware every step of the way through this process. Learning from my mistake, I was able to catch one later down the road and steer the primary author in a different direction.

2   If it looks suspicious, it probably is. I've been published in legit jour-
    nals that have horrendous websites, but it's because they don't have the
    support of a major publisher to assist them.
3   Check that the journal is indexed in one or more of the main databases.
    If it's not, then it's probably not considered legitimate by the database
    hosts, and no one will likely see or read your article anyway. Google
    Scholar is not a main database. It's not hard to get an article listed in it,
    and it looks good in the publisher's index list, but don't be fooled.
4   Check for inconsistencies and errors. Sometimes things are presented
    differently in different areas of the publisher's website. Sometimes
    links don't work. They are becoming much more clever now, but some
    irregularities might remain. It's a clue.
5   Look for the editor's information and see what you can find about him or
    her on search engines. Is the editor established in the field? What has he
    or she published? Most editors should have established themselves in the
    field to have the expertise and authority to accept or reject manuscripts.
6   How does the journal accept manuscripts? Be much more careful if
    manuscripts are sent through a webpage form or via e-mail. Most jour-
    nals have an elaborate online submission system. Again, some legiti-
    mate journals do require you to e-mail them the manuscript, but it's
    another sign to compile with the rest.
7   The Open Access fee is unusually excessive. Recognize that there are
    journals, especially in exercise science, that do have very high fees and
    are completely legitimate journals, but it's just part of that field. Often-
    times those journals expect the university or scientific institution to
    front the cost, not the author. However, beyond perhaps a few hundred
    dollars for an article to get published, you should be wary. If points 1–6
    raise some questions, and the journal is asking for a significant sum to
    publish, then you should probably be avoiding the journal.
8   The review process is exceptionally quick. Some journals take *forever*
    to get reviews in, but most do so within a month or two. Many preda-
    tory journals attract you with the speedy review process. Speedy is
    good, but not if it's too good to be true.
9   If somehow, for some reason, points 1–8 don't work and your manuscript
    is accidentally submitted to a predatory journal, expect the peer review
    process to be oddly without much content revision. That's because the
    journal doesn't really have experts in the field reviewing your work.
    Rather, any revisions will likely be grammatical or formatting. That
    should be concerning because you need the input of other experts to better
    your work. Most journals don't release who reviewed your work, but they
    often put up a list of reviewers or advisors to the journal. It's worth check-
    ing it out to make sure that you recognize some names in your field.

Pay to publish

Traditionally, publishers did not expect payment to publish journal articles. Their revenue came through university and library subscriptions, but the model is slowly changing. More and more publishers are tagging on fees to their journals. There are some stigmas associated with paying to publish, but it's largely due to predatory journals. Some highly respected journals across all of the sport, health, education, and kinesiology fields charge a publishing fee. Some even charge to submit to the journal, which makes authors think twice about whether their article would be a good fit.

Don't make the assumption that paying to publish makes your work something less than it is. In fact, some high-tier journals expect all of the work submitted to them to be externally funded through grants; in this case, a fee would be easy to cover. It's becoming part of the process, although there are still many journals that do not charge. As a personal preference, I don't like paying to publish because the fees generally come from my own pocket or my professional development fund provided by my institution. However, there are times when I do willingly pay if the manuscript has been accepted to a high-tier journal. In my opinion, it's worth the investment for the increased visibility it will gain. Sometimes a university (even as a graduate student) can and will help to cover the costs if the administration believe that it will help to improve your and their visibility. It's always worth asking.

11 Components of the submission and the submission process

Most journals have migrated to an online submission in which the software will guide you through the process quite seamlessly. Some journals still require you to do something different such as e-mail the manuscript to the editor directly, but this is becoming less and less common. I even remember one journal requiring that I print a hard copy and mail it in a manila envelope (and the journal headquarters were overseas!).

Manuscript submission requirements can usually be found on the journal's website. There is generally an "Instructions for Authors" tab or link, or something similar. It's very important to read this carefully, as many journals have their own bizarre idiosyncrasies that have to be followed before the editor will send the manuscript out for review. If you don't follow these guidelines, the editor can unsubmit your manuscript and ask you to resubmit it, or they may just reject it. Either way, it's going to delay the process. Remember that preparing the manuscript right the first time is likely going to put the editor in a better frame of mind from the outset.

The cover letter

There are generally three things that should be prepared in advance before submitting your manuscript: title page, manuscript, and cover letter. For more information about the title page, refer to Chapter 3. The cover letter is a general letter to the editor that includes a few standard sentences to explain what your manuscript is, that you've done the research ethically, and that you're not simultaneously submitting the manuscript somewhere else. It's not always a requirement, as some software requires you to click some checkboxes that state the same things, but I usually include my cover letter anyway. I've provided an example cover letter at the end of this section, and you're welcome to copy it and edit it as needed.

Tip: I highly recommend digging up the information of the editor (sometimes there is more than one) and addressing the letter directly to him or her. It personalizes the letter and allows the editor to understand that you've done your homework and have specifically targeted this journal. Editor information is usually available on the journal's website.

Dear Dr. (Editor Last Name),

Please find attached my/our article titled, "Impact of Manuscript Rejection Rate on Author Perceived Competence." This manuscript represents results of original work that have not been published elsewhere and are not part of a larger study. This manuscript has not and will not be submitted for publication elsewhere until a decision is made regarding its acceptability for publication in (*Name of Journal*). If accepted for publication, it will not be published elsewhere.

We believe that our study highlights some important findings that may be of interest to your readership and fits within the scope of your journal. We welcome your comments and suggestions.

Sincerely,
Timothy Baghurst (and additional authors)

You might also use the cover letter to justify anything particularly special about the article. For example, Jason recently had an article published as a "Rapid Report," meaning the journal goes through an extra effort of soliciting quick reviews and publishing it very quickly. He felt the article was high impact, but more importantly, he also felt he was in a race with a few other labs that could potentially be working on something similar. Therefore, explaining that to the editor helped justify it as a rapid report.

Preparing the manuscript

There are a few things I highly recommend doing to prepare the manuscript before you submit it. First, add line numbers to your manuscript even if this is not required by the journal. As a reviewer, it can be very time consuming and frustrating having to indicate to the author where something specific needs to be fixed (e.g., page 7, second paragraph, second line in paragraph). Imagine doing that for 30 items! Therefore, I recommend adding lines to your manuscript. Some journals will automatically do this for you, but some don't, and even those that do rarely match their lines with your lines. Here's how you make your reviewer think positively of your manuscript from the outset. How to do this will depend on your version of Microsoft Word, but you need to add line numbers to your manuscript. Use the "Help" function in Word to find it, but in the 2010 version, you simply go to the Page Layout tab, click on Line Numbers, and select Continuous. Continuous is very important because it removes the necessity for the reviewer to indicate the page number for each comment.

Second, remove identifiers from your manuscript. Even though you don't have your name on the manuscript, the file can still be identified, and it needs to be scrubbed of identifiers. If the journal converts your file to a pdf, then it's not a problem, but if it doesn't, then in theory, someone might be able to determine who worked on it. To remove identifiers, and again this will differ by Word version, click on the Review function in Word, click the Track Changes dropdown button and click Change User Name. You should be able to see a User Name and Initials. Mine currently displays my name and initials, so I would need to change that to something such as Anonymous and click OK to remove my contact information. Note that this isn't necessary if the journal doesn't blind the reviewers to the identity of the authors. Some journals directly identify the authors (and sometimes reviewers!) up front. However, if it is double blind (i.e., the reviewers don't know who wrote it, and you don't know who reviewed it), then submitting it without identifying marks becomes more important.

Third, make sure that your formatting follows the journal's guidelines. Remember each journal has its own idiosyncrasies, and it's important to follow their protocol.

> Tip: I download a copy of a recent article from the journal in addition to reading the author guidelines so that I can visually see the layout. Although it won't be exactly the same as your submission, you can see how the abstract is laid out, use of indents, reference style, and so on.

Fourth, make sure that headings are not presented at the very end of a page with no text underneath. If they are, then just move them down to begin at the top of the next page. References generally *do not* need to begin on a separate page, but tables and figures do (see Chapter 9 as a reminder).

Submitting the manuscript

Okay, you're ready to go. You should have everything you need to get the manuscript submitted in one attempt. There are a few different programs designed for submitting manuscripts, so while each one is different, I'm going to take you through the "typical" submission process. Assuming that you're going to be submitting the manuscript using online software, you should find a link within the author instructions to go to the submission process. Once there, you'll need to register.

Tip: I like to use the same e-mail, username, and password for all my submissions. It saves trying to remember what username and password goes to which journal.

This will require some basic information from you. You may also need to provide some keywords. In general, this information can be used by the editor to solicit you to review a manuscript for the journal, for example. You may also be asked to indicate dates when you might or might not be available. However, you'll only need to fill in the information required by the journal. Everything else you can just leave blank.

Tip: I recommend using a generic e-mail address that you will always have. Workplace and school e-mail addresses are sometimes cancelled when you leave, which could inhibit someone from being able to reach you once you've moved.

Once you have registered with the journal, you will be able to log in to the journal's main page. You may be asked how you want to log in (i.e., as an editor, reviewer, or author), and of course, you select author. Once you have logged in, you'll see several headings, probably something similar to "New Submissions," "Revisions," and "Completed." Within these headings are sometimes subheadings related to the stage that your manuscript is at in the overall process. Eventually, you want to see your manuscript in the "Completed" section.

Somewhere you should see the link to begin a new manuscript. Often you will be asked to provide information concerning what type of manuscript it is, such as a brief report, book review, research article, special feature, or whatever the editor sets up. This is followed by the title, author information, category, abstract, keywords, cover letter, reviewers, files, and anything else that the journal wants from you.

All of these items may appear in different orders, but they're generally laid out in the same or a very similar format. The title and abstract just need to be pasted from your manuscript. However, remember that journals often limit the length of both title and abstract, and the software will check their length to make sure it conforms to their specifications. You will also need to add in your authors and their relevant information. This is a pretty straightforward process, especially if you acquired all their information in advance as recommended in Chapter 3. Before moving on, be sure to check that the order of your authors is correct and that the correct person has been identified as the corresponding author (probably you, but it doesn't have to be). The corresponding author is the person who will receive all correspondence from the journal. Sometimes the journal will contact all authors, but this isn't always the case, and there will always be a point person.

You may also be asked to indicate what category or journal the manuscript is being submitted to. This option exists if the publishing company has multiple journals and uses the same system for all of them. Simply choose your journal and continue. Depending on the journal, you may be allowed to enter your keywords already created, or you may have to select from standard options. If you're not allowed to enter your own, then select the keywords most similar to the keywords that you originally chose.

As stated previously, some journals require a cover letter and others leave it optional. I always include a cover letter; it's the polite thing to do, in my opinion, and if the journal does not have a cover letter section in the submission process, they will usually have a comment section where you can include it. Whether you attach the cover letter or paste it into a section depends on the journal. Either way, you've already written it, so it's a painless task.

Some journals will ask you to include one or more recommended reviewers. To this day, I'm not entirely sure why this is done. I've known of editors who use those recommendations and those that don't, citing that most recommendations are colleagues or friends. I've also heard that it's to ensure that you, as the author, are aware of other professionals in the field.

Although entering the name of a reviewer sometimes looks like it's a required field, usually you don't have to enter any reviewers and can simply continue with the next step. If you do have to enter reviewers, it's never an easy thing. I tend to choose people I know, but also those who are going to be helpful in providing a review. I don't want a "Tim's my friend so accept as is" kind of attitude because manuscripts are generally improved with an outsider's view. From my perspective, I see little point in requesting reviewers, but some journals do expect it.

Tip: If I recommend someone to review my manuscript, I send that individual an e-mail to let him or her know that they might be receiving a request to review from the manuscript. I think it's a courtesy to do so, although technically, the manuscript is no longer blind.

Some journals may also ask you if there are any reviewers or associate editors that you do *not* want to be part of your manuscript. I've never had to address this issue (and you shouldn't either as a first-time author), so you can generally skip this part and move on.

Some journals will ask you for ancillary information, such as the number of tables and figures in the manuscript, the length of the manuscript, whether the study was funded by a grant, and other questions that can generally be quickly answered. They may also require you to check agreement to ethical statements that you may have already addressed in the cover letter.

Attaching files is usually one of the very last things that you have to do. Generally, you can attach the manuscript, a title page, figures, and tables. Sometimes journals will request additional information such as the cover letter, supplementary files, and copyright forms. For most journals, all you need to include (unless specified) are the title page, which is usually not for review, and the manuscript itself. Tables and figures are already in your manuscript and don't need to be attached separately.

Once you have attached the necessary files, continue with the next step. The software will build your file and require you to approve it. Generally, you have to approve both the html and pdf versions. Don't waste your time checking the html version. Just open it and close it. The pdf file is the one that will be sent to reviewers, so you need to check the layout to make sure that it looks the way it should. There shouldn't need to be any additional edits, but reading through the manuscript one last time is always recommended. Any symbols or special characters that you use are the most susceptible to an error during the conversion to pdf, so pay special attention to those.

Tip: When I open the pdf of my submission, I always save a copy in the folder I've created for that journal and label it "Submitted Manuscript." Then, if I get the opportunity to revise the manuscript, I'm able to quickly see what the editor/reviewer is commenting on based on what page and line number they have indicated. If I rely on my original Word document, then when I work on the document the page and line numbers are going to differ to what the reviewer is referring to. This quickly becomes very confusing! Keeping an original submitted manuscript allows you to quickly check what the reviewer was addressing.

Once you have viewed both the html and pdf versions, you should be able to submit your manuscript for the editor's consideration. If you're the corresponding author, you should also receive an e-mail confirming your submission. Now you wait!

Keeping track of the manuscript

Most journal submissions are now electronic, which provides you with an opportunity to monitor what stage your manuscript is in. Although not always true, usually the better the quality of journal, the better the information provided to you and the more accurate the updates. This is likely because the journal has a paid editor and perhaps staff to stay on top of things. Other journals may rely on the kindness of an academic doing the work in their spare time, which means you're far less likely to get updates.

In my opinion, tracking the article has little value in general, as typically information isn't updated regularly. The only time when this may be useful is if you notice that the manuscript hasn't been placed under review following a significant period of time. If that happens, there's nothing wrong with a polite e-mail to the editor asking whether the article is being reviewed. Chances are it is, and the editor just forgot to update the process online.

12 Rejection, revisions, and acceptance

The wait

When you've submitted a manuscript, you should expect to wait a while for the outcome. How long simply depends on the journal, but also what time of year it is. For example, submitting a manuscript in May could lead to delays, as many reviewers take vacations in the summer. In general, I would expect to wait for three months before considering contacting the journal. I've had manuscripts with a response within a few weeks, but I've also had to wait two years!

You may be hesitant about contacting the editor regarding your manuscript. If you appear pushy, you might think that he or she may be more inclined to reject your manuscript. Yet, I recommend sending a brief e-mail to the editor if, having waited for three months, you haven't received any communication from the journal. Sometimes mistakes do happen (they really do), and contacting them at least provides you with peace of mind that it's under review and not lost or forgotten. Here's an example e-mail:

Dear Dr. (Name of Editor):

I would be grateful if you would provide me with an update regarding manuscript number (*enter number*) with title (*enter title*). The manuscript was submitted for consideration on (*date*), and I would appreciate it if you would bring me up to date on its progress.

Sincerely,
Tim Baghurst

The three outcomes

Every journal is different, but there are typically three different outcomes from your submission: outright rejection, resubmission with revisions, and accept as is. In this next section, I'll break down what you need to do in each situation.

1. Rejection

Rejection is never something that one likes to experience, but it's going to happen. In this section, I will be presenting several rules that you should follow when you do have your manuscript rejected. However, before doing so, I wanted to at least provide you with an example of what a rejection letter, which usually comes in the form of an e-mail, will look like. They all vary, but in general, the editor will provide an overview of why he or she decided to reject the manuscript followed by the reviewer's comments. Sometimes, these comments will be written in paragraph form and at other times, it will be presented as a line-by-line explanation. In addition, some journals will provide you a numerical score on specific items such as relevance, methodology, clarity of writing, adherence to the journal's submission guidelines, and so on. It really depends on the editor and journal. That being said, here's a typical layout that I've made up:

Date

Dear Dr. Baghurst:

I write you regarding manuscript #TOEL4532 titled "Sport Performance Following the Consumption of a Complex Carb Meal" submitted to the *Journal of Sports Performance and Nutrition.* In view of the feedback from two reviewers found at the bottom of this letter, your manuscript has been declined for publication in the *Journal of Sports Performance and Nutrition.*

Both reviewers were concerned by your small sample size as well as the study's applicability to our readership. Please see the reviewers' comments to guide your future writing.

Thank you for considering the *Journal of Sports Performance and Nutrition* for the publication of your research. I hope the outcome of this specific submission will not discourage you from the submission of future manuscripts.

Sincerely,
Dr. Ura Rejected
Editor, *Journal of Sports Performance and Nutrition*

Reviewers' Comments to Author:
Reviewer 1:
Comments:
Reviewer 2:
Comments:

Rules of rejection

There are some general rules that I recommend you follow if your manuscript is rejected. Rule number one is that you should get used to being rejected. Rejection isn't fun. If you've read the preface to my book, then you'll understand what it means to be really, really rejected on a manuscript. Moreover, don't think for a minute that one day you'll suddenly have everything accepted on your first attempt or that you're never going to be rejected anymore. Bizarrely, I received a rejection e-mail while I wrote this section, and its contents weren't pretty! There have been many, many manuscripts since my first attempt, and I'm still getting rejected, and it still hurts. A colleague of mine recently submitted a document for external review that had been extensively worked on for over a year. It was a substantial document and was completely trashed by the reviewers. The document was re-written to their specifications, but it was rejected again, this time with different reasons for rejection. It was hard to see this colleague in tears after having spent countless hours trying to get the document right. Nevertheless, it happens.

Second, you should understand that it's nothing personal (usually). I'm not going to declare that some editors and reviewers aren't petty and unprofessional, but for the vast majority of submissions, the editor doesn't know you, the reviewers are blind, and they're just doing their job. That has to be understood. It's so easy to make reviews personal because, in essence, these people are questioning the very quality of your work. If you've spent years working on a project and then two or three unknown people decide that your efforts are pathetic . . . well, that hurts.

However, so many factors might come into play when a review occurs. For example, your reviewers/editor may have had a bad day, the editor may have reached his or her limit of accepted articles for that period, the journal may have just accepted a similar manuscript, or perhaps the manuscript just wasn't a great fit for the journal. All these things happen, and as a result, your manuscript was rejected, even though it may have been really good. Jason once heard someone compare the reviewer selection process to bobbing for apples blindfolded. You have no idea what you're going to get beforehand; the apple may be sour or it may be sweet. Getting good or bad reviewers is sometimes just the luck of the draw.

The third rule is to keep calm. We receive rejection in a clinical manner via e-mail, and it's easy to get angry and offended. I've no doubt that some authors who received one of my manuscript reviews were offended. I wasn't attempting to offend, but words on a page can be misunderstood and taken out of context. Understand that whatever has been written is just an opinion, and there may have been reason that the reviewer misunderstood or got something wrong. Whatever you do, don't lash out!

This comes to my fourth rule, which is contact the editor. Wait, what? Contact the editor? Well, yes, it's something I recommend. Note that I didn't say contact the editor and berate them on their ineptitude. Rather, I highly recommend that you reply to the editor thanking them for their willingness to review the manuscript and asking them to pass on your thanks to the reviewers. You see, whatever our field of expertise, it's smaller than we think it is, and there's no telling what may transpire in future. That pleasant e-mail in the face of rejection may one day reap benefits.

I recently thanked an editor, even though rejected, and I received a very friendly e-mail in return thanking me for understanding his position. Apparently, he didn't get many thank-yous for rejections, and perhaps, when he's on the search committee of a job I'm applying for (hypothetically of course), he'll remember my attitude at that time. Conversely, if I contact an editor and berate him or her, chances are that I'll never, ever be published in that journal, and there's no telling what damage such behavior could have on that job application! The reason I recommend contacting the editor is simply because I've been on the both sides of this situation. As an editor or associate editor, wouldn't it be nice to receive pleasant e-mails from people? Wouldn't that be remembered?

There may be exceptions to contacting an editor just to say thank you. At times, and they should probably be rare, you may want to "discuss" your manuscript. Personally, I've only done it twice, oddly enough both in the past year, and I'll explain why.

Tip: Recognize that in a technological age, there is opportunity to respond to the editor's e-mail quickly without too much thought. Never, ever immediately reply to such a rejection letter without sleeping on it first. It's too easy to make a hasty decision that has long-term consequences. Getting a second opinion from a colleague or trustworthy (unbiased) friend is also helpful.

In the first situation, the editor had rejected my manuscript, criticizing items associated with its lack of instrument validity and reliability. Because I didn't quite understand exactly what the editor was rejecting it for, I wrote to the editor, thanked her for the reviews, and asked her if she would be kind enough to provide further explanation of her primary concern. She did, and I was shocked when she ended up asking me to resubmit it on the condition that I fix the issues she had identified. I'd like to say that this was a fairytale ending, but it wasn't, and my manuscript eventually got rejected. However, that's not the point. Seeking clarification got me a second chance.

In the second instance, I was upset. I had submitted what I believed was a very good manuscript to a journal for which I regularly review submissions.

However, I received a rejection letter from the associate editor along with comments from two reviewers. Both reviewers spoke highly of the manuscript, but thought that it should be cut down to a brief report rather than a full-length manuscript, yet the associate editor rejected it? I didn't understand. Thus, after sleeping on it and speaking to my co-authors to solicit their input, I wrote to the associate editor and politely expressed my disappointment at the decision considering the recommendations of the reviewers. The associate editor didn't back down from his decision, but I left the situation feeling better than if I hadn't at least opened a dialogue.

Rule number four is not to give up. I've seen it happen, and it irks me. Unless the research design/purpose is simply awful (i.e., it contains a fatal flaw), a manuscript can always be improved, and there is always another journal that might be interested in what you've produced. To give you an example, last year I had a manuscript accepted to a top-tier journal in my field: it had been rejected by six other journals before it was accepted.

The fifth rule is take advantage. If you've been rejected, usually the editor will provide a strong rationale for justifying this rejection. It's not always the case, and sometimes they'll just reject you without clearly stating why. However, for the most part, you're going to get some information that you can use to better your manuscript. Recognize that each time you get a rejection is an opportunity to eliminate problems with your manuscript.

> Tip: Remember that you're not going to submit your work back to that journal, so you're not obligated to make the changes that they want. Reviewers/editors are human, and sometimes their recommendations won't better the manuscript.

I've never had a manuscript accepted to a specific journal that shall remain nameless. I've lost count how many times I've submitted there, and they have a very high rejection rate. At times, I've wondered whether it was personal, but I don't care even if it is. You see, each time I send them my manuscript and it gets rejected, I receive quality feedback. Literally, every time I've sent something for their consideration, they have responded with extremely helpful comments that have served to improve my work. Consequently, even though I didn't get into their journal (and maybe one day I will!), they have helped me get published in others. Rejections can have value.

2. Resubmission with revisions

It's a good day if you receive a letter or e-mail from the editor to inform you that your manuscript has been accepted, pending revisions (recognize that this doesn't guarantee eventual acceptance). You've made it through the second obstacle (first being that the editor was willing to send it out for review). What this essentially means is that the journal will publish your manuscript on the condition that you meet any stipulations set out by the reviewers and/or editors. These can be considered major or minor. Major revisions might require you to re-analyze aspects of the data, re-write large portions of the manuscript, add in further literature, or whatever the editor decides equates to major revisions. Minor revisions typically require fixing items such as typos, clarifying a point, finding an additional reference, or reformatting a table, for example.

When you receive your letter/e-mail from the editor, it will contain reviews just like when a manuscript is rejected. The difference this time is that you are being permitted to fix your manuscript based on the reviewer's comments. This is not an easy task, particularly if they are major revisions. I know of some authors who have not resubmitted a manuscript because they perceived the major revisions required too much effort. This is a mistake. You've completed two of the three major hurdles and to give up now doesn't make sense. Yes, your manuscript may require an overhaul, but both the editor and reviewers approve of your study despite their concerns. If it's a revision, it can be fixed, so don't quit on the process.

When you revise your manuscript, the editor will provide you with instructions on how to do so. For example, some require you to use track changes and show exactly where all your edits were made. This is unusual, however, and most will simply ask you to create a new document explaining how you addressed each comment. I like to create a new document, and at the top, I write a brief note thanking the reviewers for their time and effort in improving the manuscript and that I have addressed their concerns individually. It's a nice way to get the reviewers on your side. Then I paste all the comments into it, fix the "easy" ones first such as typos, before moving on to the more complicated issues. However, how you do it is entirely up to you, but you do need to address all of the comments even if it's just writing "fixed as requested" after a suggestion. This document will be submitted along with your revised manuscript when you resubmit it.

There are five points that need to be made regarding resubmissions: (1) reviewers are sometimes different for each revision, (2) reviewers differ in opinions, (3) you don't have to agree, (4) you can still get rejected, and (5) you still have to be patient.

1   Understand that you may not get the same reviewer during a resubmission. Ideally, you do, you've made the revisions they requested, and everyone is happy. But it doesn't always work out that way. I, unfortunately, once had to revise a manuscript four times because the reviewers kept changing. Each time we submitted, the reviewers wanted

revisions that we had made previously, and we kept going back and forth. Really, the editor should have seen what was going on and fixed it, but the multiple reviewers meant continual dissatisfaction.

2   Reviewers are human beings. Consequently, they have their own opinions about your manuscript and may or may not agree with each other. Recognize that they may have varying backgrounds and at times provide you with two recommendations for the same revision that are very different. It's rare, but once a reviewer wanted edits so contrary to my work that I wrote to the editor and politely expressed my concern with addressing any of their suggestions. The editor concurred and asked me to address only the other reviewer's concerns. I've even had reviewer comments that were opposite and mutually exclusive. In other words, no matter what, one reviewer was going to be happy and one was going to be upset. In these cases, I add a comment in my cover letter (or send a separate e-mail to the editor) informing them that it is impossible to make them all happy, but I did the best I could.

3   Because reviewers are humans, and therefore subject to their own viewpoint, you don't always have to agree with them. When it comes to minor formatting and editing issues, I wouldn't disagree. What's the point? However, let's say that hypothetically one reviewer really doesn't like the statistical procedure you used and wants you to rerun the data using a different procedure. Does this mean that you have to do it their way? Absolutely not! The key here is determining whether the reviewer is correct, or perhaps more correct than you. You are entitled to disagree with the reviewer. However, if/when you do, be respectful (they can still reject you), and clearly explain why you disagree with their recommendation. Citing a reference or two to back up your rebuttal would help in this case.

4   As I just mentioned, a manuscript that is accepted pending revisions can still be rejected! I've been fortunate not to have experienced this, but a colleague of mine recently did, and it was incredibly frustrating. After making major revisions to the manuscript, which took considerable time and effort, it was sent out for review again and rejected. Therefore, I can't stress that while you've overcome another obstacle in getting another opportunity to make revisions, there's still one more to go. Don't celebrate too much yet! Why can a manuscript be rejected? Well, you may have been careless in the revisions or been unable to fix what the reviewer expected you to fix. I mentioned in (1) that reviewers change and that this could affect the outcome. I was recently asked to review a resubmission that I had not originally reviewed. I had expected to simply read it and check that the author had addressed the necessary reviews, but I ended up recommending rejecting the manuscript due to its many faults.

5 You still have to be patient. A revision can take just as long to be reviewed as the original manuscript. Add in multiple revisions (hopefully not!), and you can see why a manuscript might take years to be accepted. I generally contact the editor a couple of months following the resubmission, particularly if the resubmission required only minor edits, to check the status of the manuscript.

As mentioned previously, it's important to always be respectful when responding to reviewers. In fact, it doesn't hurt to stroke their ego a little along the way. My co-author, Jason, has a system that was taught to him, which he now teaches to his graduate students, and he never strays from. It's a system very similar to my own. He opens a separate document, copies and pastes the reviewer comments into it, and addresses each and every comment one-by-one. This document will be attached separately as "Responses to Reviewers" in the resubmission. Before any of the comments are addressed, he first states to the reviewers:

> Thank you all for your thoughtful and thorough reviews. We feel that we adequately addressed your concerns, and in doing so, have significantly improved the quality and clarity of the manuscript. Below are all the comments, as well as our point-by-point responses in red italics.

This note at the beginning is respectful, shows gratitude, and makes the reviewers feel like their work has made a significant contribution. Second, he provides a positive comment or repeats his gratitude in his point-by-point responses. He also points them to the exact place in the manuscript the revision takes place (when possible). Here are a few examples of responses to reviewer comments:

- "This is a great point and our revised manuscript has been modified to reflect this. In the 2nd paragraph of our discussion, we have added . . ."
- "Thank you for your comment. As requested, the following statement has been added to the methods on page 7, line 25 . . ."
- "Thank you for your comment. While we understand your point, we respectfully disagree with . . ." (*Again, if you're going to do a rebuttal instead of a revision, be sure to justify your stance.*)

3. Accept as is

If you receive this from the editor, it's time to party! Your manuscript has been accepted, and it will be scheduled for publication. I have only ever received this once with a first-time submission. Generally, at least one revision is required. You may still be asked to review a proof copy of the manuscript to double check everything, but this is a formality, and only typo errors are typically corrected at this stage.

How long you have to wait until your manuscript is accepted varies. Online, open access journals tend to be much quicker, as there are less printing/publishing requirements. In general, you should expect to see your manuscript published within a year, but in the past, I have had to wait more than two years to see my article in press. Either way, once the manuscript has been accepted by the editor, it can be considered "in press" and can be cited in future work.

13 Presentations

Consider this a bonus section. Several years ago, when I was a relative greenhorn in the academic community, I attended a national conference associated with my field of expertise. Bright-eyed, I went to presentations intent on learning from the greats in my discipline. I don't remember the presentations for their content, unfortunately, but for the horrific nature in which some were presented. I'm talking about red text on a blue background, typos galore, font too small to read, and so on. It was awful, and I was so disappointed by the poor quality that I wrote to the organization and asked if I could present on presenting at the next conference. They agreed, and I did so a year later.

I tell this story to highlight that poor presenting skills exist at the highest level and that content can get lost in the presentation itself. Therefore, I'm going to provide several pointers to make sure that your presentation enhances your content and doesn't hinder it.

General guidelines

I adhere to the KISS principle. Most people refer to it as Keep It Short Stupid, but that's not how I use it. KISS to me refers to Keep It Short and Sweet (or Short and Simple). Rarely will you have an audience complain that your presentation was too short, but often an audience will get itchy if it's too long.

You need to use one or two slides for each idea or topic. There's no need to provide reams and reams of text or slides. To cut down your chance of reading the content, don't write the content in sentence form. Rather, provide bullet points. Really, the slides are there to remind you what to talk about. If they included all of the information, then what value do *you* have? Instead, a few bullets per slide provides you with reminders about what's important for your audience to understand.

Tip: Always, always have a backup of your presentation in some format. I always have one on a flash drive, e-mail a copy to myself, and have a copy in Dropbox (www.dropbox.com). Most conference locations will have wi-fi that will enable you to still access the presentation if you lose the flash drive or if it becomes corrupted.

Slide design, background, and layout

It's easy to mess this up, and most people go too far. Consequently, your background can look completely hideous and totally distract from what you're trying to say. Use dark colors, and the text can easily get lost in the background. Thus, try not to use bizarre colors that you stopped using in grade school. Instead, recognize that white is good, and use a clean, simple background. It's okay to have a little color in the background/design, and many PowerPoint backgrounds have a little color on the sides or corners, but the entire slide is not a good idea. You don't know the quality of the projector or screen you might have, so err on the side of caution.

Tip: I recommend testing your slides on a projector before your official presentation. This will help to ensure that your slides are bright enough and that the text is easy to read. Also, if presenting a poster, remember that white is cheaper to print!

Font size and type

There are times when you feel that all your work absolutely must be included in your presentation or poster because it is *so* important! This often occurs when you have a paragraph (e.g., from a paper) that is so beautifully succinct and detailed that you cannot bear to cut it down or split it up. There is no doubt that it can be extremely difficult to cut down what you see as vital information. Unfortunately, what you viewed as a work of literary art will not be appreciated by the masses flocking to your presentation or the curious seeking out your poster. The reality is that although a small font size like this allows you to pack in a great number of words that you think are absolutely vital, most of us haven't reached this point in your supposedly flowing prose. If we have, then we're either ultra-dedicated or slightly insane, or we're so bored with what you're talking about that we'd rather read this very, very long sentence just to keep our minds occupied. By this point, you've lost our concentration, and we're not going to be appreciating your literary talents.

There's another issue with small font sizes. As a presenter, you might actually end up reading it out loud yourself and not facing the audience! How many times have you heard the presenter say, "I'm sorry it's so difficult to read" when they see their presentation appear on the screen? Therefore, here are a few tips to make sure that this doesn't happen to you!

Remember that your job is to present, not to read. If you've a lot of text on the slide, then you're more likely to read it rather than talk about it. Less is sometimes more, and it relates to both presentations and posters. We have a habit of wanting to include as much text as possible, but by doing so, we begin to shrink the size of the font. Big mistake.

For presentations, use a typical PowerPoint size font or larger. For posters, it will depend on the size of the poster. However, if you've made your poster using PowerPoint, you can print a test page, and it will display the actual size of the text. I really don't recommend anything under size 32, but also recognize that each font's size is actually a different size (i.e., 12 font Arial does not equal 12 font Adobe Arabic).

With respect to fonts, use sans serif fonts such as Arial, Century Gothic, and Verdana. These are all very visually pleasing fonts that are easy to read on a screen. Don't choose anything unusual. Remember that for most presentations, you're not using your tablet/laptop. Thus, if that laptop doesn't have your Radiohead font (yes, there is such a font), your font isn't going to load. The results won't be pretty!

Bullets

Bullets are a good thing, but they can also damage your presentation. They can serve to keep content limited on a slide, but the danger is placing too many bullets on one slide. Thus,

- Don't
- Use
- Too
- Many
- Bullets
- Per
- Slide
- As
- You
- Will
- End
- Up
- Losing
- The

- Key
- Point
- That
- You
- Are
- Conveying

Typos

Typos are a pet peeve of mine. It drives me crazy to see typos in anything (hopefully none in this book!). There are few things more distracting in a presentation than a big, fat typo staring at you for five minutes while the presenter talks. To me, typos imply the following:

1   Quick, I have to prepare something for this presentation I totally forgot about!
2   It's only a presentation, nothing important, so I don't need to be too careful.
3   If I'm this careless in my presentation of the material, you have no idea what I did in the research I'm presenting!
4   I forgot to spell cheek, and my work is ful of miss tacks.

To avoid typos, I recommend that you proofread the presentation your-self aloud. Also, remember to run spellcheck, as it may pick up one or two things that you missed. Finally, ask someone whose opinion you trust to proof it also. Once, when I returned an assignment to one of my students that was full of typos, his response was "But my English high school teacher proofed it for me!" Well, that teacher may have not had time to do a good job, or, shudder to think, was a poor English teacher. The point is that it has to be someone who's going to do a great job, not someone who you ask just because of his or her status or convenience.

Graphs and graphics

Have you ever been to a presentation or seen a poster that was just reams and reams of text? Boring right? I'm all for graphs and graphics as long as they're presented appropriately (see Figures 13.1 and 13.2). Two general rules are that you should fit the picture/graph in the appropriate location and avoid using small image files. With respect to pictures, always try to include high-resolution pictures. The problem with small pictures is that when you enlarge them, they pixelate into something unrecognizable. Then when you present them on a large screen . . . well, you get the picture (pun intended).

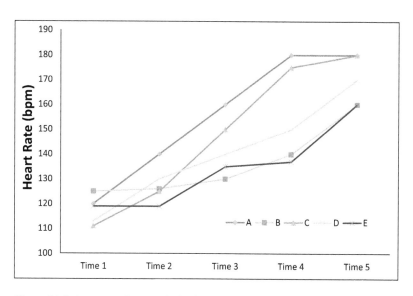

Figure 13.1 An appropriate graph that is easy to follow and read

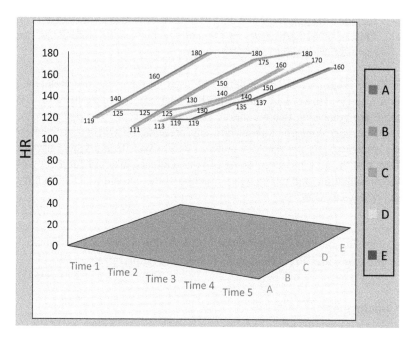

Figure 13.2 The same variables presented in a cluttered and confusing manner

Researching layout and referencing

I don't know why. but some presenters decide not to follow typical research layouts or formatting. Most people attending your presentation will be comfortable with reading and seeing a specific format. This could be MLA, APA, AMA, Harvard, Vancouver, Chicago (CMS), or some other style. Doesn't it make sense to present using the most commonly used style? Therefore, particularly if you're presenting a research study, lay it out in the manuscript style most commonly used by individuals in that profession.

References should be cited in full at the end and should follow the correct format. This isn't a time to get creative! However, within the text, you can cite three different ways. Each has a disadvantage:

1   Use numbers to indicate a reference[1] and list them at the end of your presentation. This is a great way of saving space in the presentation and not overwhelming the text with lots of authors.
    However, this means that you can't visually associate an author with a comment.
2   Use numbers to indicate a reference and include the reference as a footnote on that slide. This resolves the issues in (1), but it can make the slide look cluttered and will limit your space on each slide.
3   Include references as you would in a manuscript (e.g., Baghurst, 2017). This resolves both issues in (1) and (2), but lengthy references can really fill up a slide.

There is no perfect option here. I've used all three, but my preference is to use (3). However, I automatically switch the reference to "et al." if there are more than two authors to conserve space. It's not perfect APA, but I'm more concerned about how my presentation will be received by my audience, and not the APA police. I do always cite everything in APA format at the end, however. Some of your audience may ask for a copy of the presentation, and including this section at the end allows them to have the references also.

Tip: The shortcut for superscript is to hold down Ctrl, Shift, and + at the same time. Press them again to return to normal size.

Conclusions

Providing a summary at the end can sometimes be awkward. Imagine the awkward silence when the presenter goes from discussing a point to the dreaded black slide at the end of the PowerPoint. Instead, use a slide to summarize the main points of your presentation that suggest future avenues for research. Then, open the floor to questions (if permitted). I like to end with a slide that provides my contact information and a question mark graphic or a "Questions" heading of some kind. This allows my audience to write down my contact info while questions are ongoing. If you give a great presentation but don't provide your audience with the opportunity to contact you, you could be missing all kinds of opportunities!

14 Book publishing

If you're not skipping this section, then it means you might be thinking about publishing a book of some form. Stop and reconsider! It's not for the faint of heart. Yet, if you do persevere, it can also be a very rewarding experience; personally more so than financially. Contrary to what some might think, you're not going to make a huge amount of money from writing a book. Yes, it's possible, but you have to hit the niche market and sell *a lot* of books to really make it a true motivator. However, it's a pretty cool thing to have your work read in classrooms around the world and used by your colleagues.

Just understand this before you begin: it's a very challenging task and one I don't necessarily recommend until you are established in your career and can dedicate plenty of time to it. Some higher education institutions do not allow (or might discourage) writing a book, at least in the fields mentioned in this book anyway, until you have acquired tenure. Other disciplines (e.g., history, literature) may *expect* you to write a book before you get tenure.

All publishers are not created equal

Sometimes you'll get e-mails in your inbox from random publishers encouraging you to publish your book with them! It's flattering, but it can be a big mistake to not do your homework on them. In some situations, you may find that while the publisher will print your book, it's completely on you to write it and create the photos, graphs, table of contents, and even cover. You need to understand that you are being taken advantage of, and they're essentially exploiting your work for their gain.

Research your publisher carefully. Are they a common name in your field? Do they attend your conferences? Are they publishing a lot of material? Will they advertise it? Find out as much as possible about them before you delve into signing a contract.

Tip: If you know an author who used a publisher you're interested in working with, try to contact that author for an opinion. Just because his or her book was published doesn't mean the author was happy with the experience.

Some publishers have a lot more influence than others do, and I would caution against working with smaller publishers. Having done both, there are advantages to a smaller publisher. It's nice to have direct contact with almost everybody in the organization, and you may feel a little more special accordingly. However, usually they have a much lower budget for marketing and can't attend all the conferences or produce all the marketing materials that a larger publisher can. Conversely, a larger publisher may "lose" your book within the many, many texts they publish. Your book may be hidden at a conference because they are selling so many different titles!

Personally, I would encourage you to choose a more prominent publisher if you can, as they have the marketing experience and budget to really get your book out there. It's just too hard for smaller publishers to promote your book, even if yours is the best one they have. I strongly discourage paying to publish or self-publishing. You really do need that editing and quality control that comes with being published by someone who knows what they're doing.

Finding a publisher and editor

This sounds difficult, but it's easier than you might think. Attend a conference in your field, and you can probably pick the publishers that you should consider writing for. If they're not there, how are they going to promote your book? In fact, some publishers, even in the fields covered in this book, only publish books for *your* classes and take what they can from that. They literally don't attend conferences, send out marketing e-mails, or anything!

Once you've established who are top dogs in your field, contact them. This may be in person at a conference – you won't likely find your editor there, but the representative will be able to point you to the right person to contact – or just online. Most publishing websites will have a contact person for your discipline.

Don't expect them to contact you, especially as you're relatively new to the field. How will they know you're an expert? Rather, you need to start the conversation. Take this book, for example. Initially the conversation began when I served as an external reviewer for a textbook that Taylor & Francis published and wanted an opinion of. I began some e-mail conversations with them about a book I wanted to write for a class in which I couldn't find a good book. From that discussion, I presented this book idea, and here we are! However, without that initial discussion, Taylor & Francis and my editor would've never known my interest in writing this book or indeed my ability to write it. It required *me* making that proposal to *them*.

Review process

Before offering you a contract, the publisher will expect you to write them a proposal. Most proposals are in a specified form and ask you to include things such as the chapter outlines, competing texts, information about the author(s), and probably a sample chapter. Just as a journal would, most publishers will send your proposal out to two or three reviewers to solicit their expert opinions. They'll use this feedback to evaluate whether they want to move forward with the book and offer you a contract.

Signing the contract

Don't expect to be negotiating with the publisher; maybe much further down the road when you've established yourself as a "must read" author that might be the case, but as a younger, less experienced author, it's really up to them what you get paid. I can't give specifics, because each publisher is different, but some will set a percentage following costs, some will require *x* number sold before sending you a check, and others will set a percentage straight from the beginning. They're all unique.

> Tip: Clarify whether the book will be considered as a main text or a supplemental text. A supplemental text is often less used or considered an ancillary text and will sell fewer copies. Accordingly, the publisher may offer the author a lower percentage because they expect to sell fewer books.

Also, understand that a contract is a binding document. This seems obvious, but it holds both parties accountable. It means the publisher has obligations to help publish and promote your book, but primarily for you, it means you have specific deadlines and expectations.

Tip: When setting deadlines with the publisher, always overestimate how long it will take you to accomplish projects. Yes, it's nice to impress them with your strict deadlines, but if anything happens that prohibits work for a while, you're stuck. A little leeway really helps just in case.

How long it will take you to complete a book is very much dependent on you and how long and complicated the book is going to be. I would encourage you to solicit the advice of the editor you're working with, as they have much more experience than you on how long it takes to prepare and complete a finished product. Be aware that the publisher may set deadlines based on the academic year; they're thinking about when they need to get the book in press to make it available for a specific semester.

Contracts will differ depending on the number of authors. Some publishers will be very explicit that all authors receive an equal share of the revenue, whereas others will allow the primary author to negotiate with the other authors on revenue. For example, if you as the primary author have written the majority of the book, the publisher may allow you to work with the second author so that you receive a greater percentage of the "author" revenue.

Tip: Check with the publisher on what price they intend to sell the book at, and make sure you're happy with its estimated cost. I, unfortunately, know of an author who did not, and the book's price was set so high that no one buys it. The author's work, while published, is read by very few, and it deserves better. Unfortunately, the price was not agreed upon prior to any agreement signed, and little can be done by the author to correct that mistake.

Getting it done

A book isn't like an article. It can't be written in a few days. It's something that takes time and continual effort. Similar to a dissertation, it's an endurance race rather than a sprint, and it's something you just have to keep plugging away at even if you're not in the mood. Remember that a good editor will help you improve your work, even if it's initially bad, but an editor can't improve work that you haven't written.

Expect books revisions to come back to you more than once. It's a big undertaking, and the longer it is, the more editing that can be done to it. You may never be perfectly satisfied with the end product, but at some point, you need to approve it. Note that in some situations the editor will send the book out for external review prior to publishing. This is to ensure that it's going to receive good feedback and that small things can be fixed before going to print.

Going to press

How quickly the book is published after the final edition is complete is very much dependent on the publisher. They will have semester deadlines very much in mind, however. Recognize that each publisher will have various levels of author control over the final product. Some, as already mentioned, allow the author to do pretty much all of it, whereas others will want to do it their way based on their expertise. From personal experience, most publishers are quite amenable to collaboration to make sure that the author is satisfied. No publisher wants to get a bad reputation within the field for being difficult to work with.

Resources

American Medical Association. (2007). *AMA manual of style: A guide for authors and editors* (10th ed.). New York: Oxford University Press.

American Psychological Association. (2013). *Publication manual of the American Psychological Association* (6th ed.). Washington, D.C.: Author.

Modern Language Association. (2009). *MLA handbook for writers of research papers* (7th ed.). New York: Author.

The University of Chicago Press. (2010). *The Chicago manual of style* (16th ed.). Chicago: Author.

Index